D1527811

STUDY GUIDE TO JOHN E. H. SHERRY,

The Laws of Innkeepers, THIRD EDITION

STUDY GUIDE TO

JOHN E. H. SHERRY,

The Laws of Innkeepers,

THIRD EDITION

GWEN SEAQUIST

Cornell University Press

ITHACA AND LONDON

First published 1993 by Cornell University Press.

International Standard Book Number 0-8014-9923-2
Printed in the United States of America

⊗ The paper in this book meets the minimum requirements of the
American National Standard for Information Sciences—Permanence
of Paper for Printed Library Materials, ANSI Z39.48-1984.

Contents

[v]

Part III. Tort Law: Liability for Guest's Safety

Part IV. Responsibility for Property of Guests and Patrons

Part VII. Selected Topics

Preface

This study guide was written as a companion volume to *The Laws of Innkeepers*, third edition, by John E. H. Sherry. *The Laws of Innkeepers* is a law casebook. Although it contains a great deal of commentary and is used as a textbook for courses in hospitality law, it can be daunting to students who lack a legal background. The study guide is intended as an aid to such students—students in a nonlaw program who have never taken a law course—and as a study tool for preparing for tests. It provides explanations of concepts that are essential to an understanding of the cases and commentary in the textbook. For example, the study guide includes chapters on the court systems and civil litigation, constitutional law, and contract law. In addition, it summarizes the material in the textbook and highlights important points and cases.

How to Use the Study Guide

The study guide is intended to be used with the textbook close at hand. Regardless of which book you start with, you will find yourself going from one to the other. Because the study guide contains material not in the textbook, the study guide chapters do not correspond exactly to the textbook chapters. The table of correspondence that follows this preface will help orient you so that you can find your way around easily in both books. As the table shows, there is no study guide chapter to correspond with textbook Chapter 16. Discussion of that chapter was not included in the study guide because the material in it is more for reference than instruction.

Case citations are given in the study guide only for those cases that do not appear in the textbook.

The glossary includes terms from both the textbook and the study guide.

Wherever possible chapter titles and section headings in the study guide exactly match those in the textbook. The study guide includes, as a further aid to locating material, extensive cross-references, which warrant further comment.

Cross-references to parts of the study guide itself are to chapter or chapter and section title only. (Example: See Chapter 6, Capacity.) Cross-references to chapters or pages in the textbook specify that they are to the textbook. (Examples: See textbook, Chapter 21. See textbook, p. 38.) Cross-references to sections in the textbook are to chapter and section number only and are enclosed in parentheses. [Example: Duty to admit (3:3).] Cross-references to cases in the textbook give the case name and page number (or numbers) but no citation. [Example: . . . discrimination. *Cromwell v. Stephens* (textbook, pp. 17–20).] The name of the case cited may appear in the textbook as a heading of an excerpted case, in the text itself, or in a footnote.

Most chapters are followed by one or more review questions. These questions were designed to review the chapter material, to raise questions about it, and to test your comprehension of it. Correct answers to the questions are a good indication that you have a firm grasp of the material contained in both the study guide and the textbook.

As you begin your study of legal issues don't forget that the material in this book and the textbook is about people. Every case was someone's day in court, whether that someone was a hotelier, an injured child, or a class of people. Their stories made law, which Professor Sherry and I now share with you.

I am grateful to Harvard University Law School for its support while I was a visiting researcher there in 1990–91. Many thanks are also due to Ithaca College's School of Business for sabbatic support during the same period.

This book is affectionately dedicated to the two Dors.

GWEN SEAQUIST

Ithaca, New York

Correspondence between Study Guide and Textbook Chapters

PART I

INTRODUCTION TO THE
LAWS OF INNKEEPERS

CHAPTER 1

Introduction to Business
and Hospitality Law

Business and hospitality law, like all law, has evolved in response to society's need to create, interpret, and enforce the rights and responsibilities of individuals and organizations. Such rights and responsibilities arise out of either voluntary relationships or duties imposed by government. The law creates a system of dispute resolution that balances the rights and responsibilities of the parties concerned and imposes an appropriate legal remedy.

For example, if a hotel owner does not live up to the terms of a reservation contract recognized as a legally enforceable agreement, the guest who made the reservation may sue. If the court rules in favor of the patron, she might recover compensation in the form of damages or might be excused from meeting her own obligations in the voluntary relationship if the owner's failure to perform was substantial.

In the case of a duty imposed by government: if a local or state law requires installation of sprinkler systems and smoke detectors in all public hotel rooms, a hotelkeeper who fails to install them may be sued for personal injuries suffered by a guest who was burned in a fire made more severe by the hotel's failure to meet the governmental duty.

Why Study Business and Hospitality Law?

One of the first questions you may ask when beginning this course is how will knowledge of law be relevant to your future in the hospitality industry. After all, you may reason, if a legal problem should ever arise, it seems only prudent to immediately contact an attorney. Furthermore, one law course is not sufficient preparation for you to give legal advice. You would of course be correct on both counts. What then is the purpose of studying law at this level?

There is a growing trend in the United States to settle all matters, large and small, in court. One young woman made headlines recently when she sued her boyfriend for refusing to take her to their high school prom. That action may seem silly and eccentric, but the reality is that litigation over even trivial matters will be costly to you as a businessperson. In 1990 alone, millions of civil actions were litigated in U.S. courts, and a significant number arose in the hospitality industry. Litigation is expensive, it disrupts daily operations, it creates negative publicity, and it is stressful for all involved. To minimize the consequences of such legal liability and to reduce or eliminate the risks that may create such liability, you must be familiar with business and hospitality law.

A proactive management policy of prevention—not just a reactive policy—should be a top priority. Knowledge of the law will allow you to institute corrective measures so that you can avoid litigation.

Increasingly, plaintiffs who win lawsuits against hotels are being awarded high damages. For example, in 1989 the Las Vegas Hilton Casino was found liable in an age and sex discrimination lawsuit. The jury awarded $38,000,000 in damages to the hotel's employees for age discrimination; the judge added $1,602,882 for sex discrimination. Think of the money that could have been saved had the hotel's management corrected the discriminatory actions earlier. An additional consideration is that insurance carriers faced with paying such high damage recoveries are reluctant to continue coverage, and many have raised their premiums to impossible limits in reaction to this explosion in litigation.

Your awareness of potential legal problems may result in financial savings because you can avoid litigation and because you can obtain insurance. The alternative—expensive litigation followed by liability for which you have no insurance—is certainly a distressing situation and, unfortunately, one in which some businesses have found themselves.

In addition to the obvious issue of adverse money awards and the cost of defending many lawsuits, the adverse public image created by the news media indirectly drains income by causing past and future guests to avoid the establishment. Adverse publicity is especially damaging when a case involves injury to guests, thereby giving the general public the impression that the premises are unsafe.

Another, often overlooked, area of concern to hotelkeepers is random acts of violence. Physical damage and business interruptions are increasingly caused by major incidents such as bombings or terrorist attacks. Neither could be attributed to the actions of a hotelkeeper, but both are devastating and extremely expensive to rectify. Hospitality entities are well advised to become knowledgeable about their liability in such cases.

As if these concerns were not enough, governments at all levels are enacting new laws or amending old laws to tighten regulations and increase enforcement of security and safety in the hospitality industry. Fire protection is one clear and justifiable example.

All these pressures require an understanding of one's legal rights and responsibilities. Such an awareness enables management to prevent exposure to risks to the extent possible, rather than simply to react to the consequences on a case-by-case basis.

Common Legal Issues in the Hospitality Industry

The legal issues you will face as a manager in the hospitality industry fall into four major categories: contracts, torts, constitutional law, and employment law. Familiarizing yourself with these categories will allow you to recognize the proper area of law governing a particular event. Accordingly, you may be able to take preventive action.

CONTRACTS

In the hospitality industry issues related to contracts include the creation and termination of the innkeeper-guest relationship, rights and duties pertaining to reservations, and franchise agreements.

Consider this hypothetical situation: Sylvester Stone, a superstar, reserves a suite at the Ritz-Mayfair Hotel in Beverly Hills, and the hotel accepts his substantial deposit. Upon the date set for his arrival, Sly enters the hotel lobby without warning dressed and made up as the Phantom of the Opera, who he is portraying in a movie. If the hotel staff doesn't recognize him, is the hotel legally obligated to accept him as a guest or serve him by reason of his confirmed reservation?

TORTS

Torts are civil wrongs for which the court may award money damages. This category includes treatment of guests; responsibility for persons and property of guests; duties to nonguests; and overall liability for on-premises incidents that result in injury to persons and property, including liability for serving alcoholic beverages.

Consider these two hypothetical cases:

Mr. and Mrs. George Brown and their six-year-old daughter, Georgie, are registered guests at the High Top Family Dude Ranch in Alpine, Wyoming. The local forest ranger has warned management that dangerous grizzly bears in the immediate area have attacked humans without provocation and that guests and others must be warned not to go on trails maintained by the ranch for guest use until further notice. The ranch refuses to issue such a warning because it fears the loss of business and because no guests have ever suffered harm when such warnings given in the past were ignored. On this occasion, Georgie is walking on a hiking path within sight of her parents when she is surprised by a full-grown grizzly hidden in the undergrowth near the path. The bear charges and badly mauls Georgie before the Browns can rescue her. Is the ranch legally liable for the injuries suffered by Georgie?

The Westminister Hotel, without the knowledge or approval of the appropriate state liquor control authority, installs self-service alcoholic beverage dispensers in its guest rooms. These rooms are rented to underage high school students to enable them to attend a dance held at the hotel. The rooms are rented at the request of the parents so that the students won't have to drive at all hours of the night. No liquor sales are permitted at such dances. On this occasion, the underage students learn of the existence of the alcohol dispenser, which can be operated with the room key. After imbibing the alcohol freely, one of the students gets into an altercation with another guest, not connected with the dance, and assaults him. If it can be shown that the intoxication caused or contributed to the assault, is the hotel liable to the other guest for the sale of the alcohol to a minor and the intoxication of the minor stemming therefrom?

CONSTITUTIONAL LAW

Studying fundamental constitutional concepts leads to a discussion of laws pertaining to discriminatory behavior in the creation of the innkeeper-guest relationship and in the treatment of guests and employees. Constitutional law also includes federal and state statutes that regulate the sale of food, beverages, and intoxicants to guests, patrons, and others.

EMPLOYMENT LAW

Employment law is a rapidly growing area of law. It includes creation of the employment relationship, liability for actions of the employee, workers' compensation, and insurance matters.

Consider this hypothetical case: The Fabulous Hotel hired Michael Smith on February 15, 1989, to work as an air-conditioning mechanic. At the annual picnic in July of that year, Michael assaulted a fellow employee. Fabulous took no action. At the annual picnic the following year, Michael became noticeably intoxicated from alcohol served by the Fabulous to its employees and assaulted another employee, causing severe injuries. Did the hotel condone Michael's conduct by allowing or ignoring such behavior on the previous occasion? Can the insurance company refuse to defend the hotel on the grounds that the hotel took no preventive action? And can the hotel fire the employee without establishing a record of behavior?

As you may note, the answers to these questions are not easy. But you may find it helpful to remember the law by pigeonholing the various cases you encounter in this course into one of these areas of law.

The Origins of Law

Before studying the major areas of law in any detail, you must first study the law from a historical perspective. Set out below are some of the origins of law. As you review these, remember that the law today is built on the laws from our past. (For further discussion see Chapter 3.)

COMMON LAW

One of the features that distinguishes the history and development of U.S. law from other systems is the reliance on judge-made law. Also known as the common law or case law, this system is created by the courts as they decide disputes brought before them.

For example, suppose that a guest of the Fabulous Hotel falls and suffers a serious injury. She decides to sue the hotel. This lawsuit is a case heard by a judge (or jury). At the conclusion of the case, the judge writes an opinion rendering a decision. This written opinion is judge-made law. The cases in the textbook are examples of someone's day in court and the judge's (or jury's) ruling on the lawsuit.

When deciding a case, the judge relies on previous similar cases or opinions. When the plaintiff in the action against the Fabulous Hotel brings her lawsuit, the judge will compare her situation with previous situations that were brought before a similar court. This is called the doctrine of *stare decisis*, which means "apply the prior legal principles found in decided cases to the current problem." As is evident, the doctrine of *stare decisis* maintains continuity; an outcome is fairly predictable when a judge relies on previous decisions to render a current decision.

In a case for which no prior legal principles exist, the judge's rule is called original rule law. The case decided becomes precedent for subsequent cases. Today, *precedent* has come to mean a singular prior decision. We might say that a case decided in 1967 is precedent for a case being decided in 1991. *Stare decisis*, then, is the use of precedent (or previous case law, judge-made law, or an opinion) to decide a case today.

This principle, however, is not and cannot be rigid. Courts must be flexible to meet new challenges and needs. If the facts on which the past rule was based are different from those of the present case, the judge will not be compelled to follow the prior law. Also, if the judge believes that the prior rule is obsolete and no longer appropriate to certain conditions, he or she is free to change the rule. In such cases the need for flexibility outweighs the need for certainty under the common law.

STATUTORY, OR LEGISLATIVE, LAW

Unlike the common law, statutory, or legislative, law is created by federal and state legislative bodies. The federal legislative body is

Congress, located in Washington, D.C. State legislative bodies are called state legislatures and are located in a state's capital. Examples of state and federal statutes appear throughout the textbook. Statutory laws are the primary source of new law and uniform economic and social change in the United States. Where the common law is too slow in changing or overruling a precedent, the legislature may intervene to accomplish change or to overturn a common-law decision that conflicts with legislative wishes. Because the common-law court can hear and decide only those cases brought before it, the legislature can create new law more rapidly to meet economic and social needs.

A good example of this is the case of *Texas v. Johnson*, 109 S. Ct. 2533 (1989), in which the U.S. Supreme Court held that the First Amendment protects protesters who burn the flag as a political demonstration. Note that this is judgemade law. Immediately following the decision, legislation was introduced to prohibit flag burning. It could take twenty or thirty years for a similar case to come before the U.S. Supreme Court again. The legislature, on the other hand, can move in weeks to create a law that overturns the decision of the court.

In the area of business or commercial law, great effort has been devoted to making a specific body of law uniform. The Uniform Commercial Code (UCC) is the most recent example. It has been adopted with variations in all fifty states to simplify, clarify, and update the law applicable to commercial transactions.

The UCC states rules governing contracts for the sale of goods. It also covers commercial paper, such as checks, and banking rules. It was written to make sales transactions between people in different states more uniform. The UCC was then sent to the individual state legislatures for adoption. Thus, although it was originally not a legislative law, when the individual legislatures passed the UCC into law, it became a state statute or state legislation.

ADMINISTRATIVE LAW

Administrative law stems from the creation of administrative agencies by governmental authority. These agencies can affect the rights of private parties by making and enforcing rules and by judging cases. Administrative law regulates such agencies in the use of powers. The purpose of such agencies is to handle, on a day-by-day basis, complex matters that require special expertise that courts and the legislature lack. Another purpose is to combine legislative, judicial, and executive governmental functions and thereby provide greater continuity at less cost to the taxpayer. Most citizens deal with administrative agencies more often than with legislative or judicial branches of the government.

One of the easiest examples of an administrative agency to understand is the FAA, or Federal Aviation Administration. Can you imagine why Congress creates federal agencies? In the case of the FAA, Congress lacks the expertise to make rules about aviation. It must therefore defer to an agency composed of individuals with that particular knowledge. Second, Congress does not have time to regulate aviation on a day-by-day basis. Congress defers its authority in other areas as well, for example, in communications (regulated by the FCC), in advertising (FTC), in food and drugs (FDA), and in taxes (IRS).

THE CONSTITUTIONAL FRAMEWORK OF LAW

All our law, whether case law, statutory law, or administrative law, is shaped by and ultimately must conform to the U.S. Constitution. The Constitution is the ultimate source of law and of all legal authority in the United States. It is the supreme law of the land. No state, federal, or other law should violate the Constitution. The final decision maker in interpreting the Constitution is the U.S. Supreme Court.

Review Questions for Chapter 1

1. Suppose that in 1984 the U.S. Supreme Court rendered a decision banning discrimination against African Americans in hotels. How do the concepts of *stare decisis* and precedent apply to this decision?

2. What are some distinctions between case law and statutory law?

3. What is the UCC? How did it become statutory law?

4. What are some of the benefits of studying law to you as a hotel management student?

5. What is the significance of judge-made law? How is it affected by legislation?

CHAPTER 2

The Court Systems
and Civil Litigation

Every state in the United States (and the District of Columbia) has a particular court system. In addition, the United States has a federal court system. As a result, the entire court system in the United States is referred to as a dual system, meaning it has two separate and distinct systems—federal and state.

As a hotelier, you will need to be familiar with the court system in your state as well as with the federal system. In particular you should be concerned with how a court is chosen and which courts hear which types of cases.

Subject-Matter Jurisdiction

THE NEW YORK STATE COURT SYSTEM

Subject-matter jurisdiction is the power of a court to hear a case. This "power" may be found in the state's constitution or in legislative law. For example, the New York State Constitution describes the New York Supreme Court as the court of "general original jurisdiction," meaning that this court has the power to hear all types of cases.

In general, courts are divided into courts of *general* versus *limited* jurisdiction and *trial* versus *appellate* courts.

General jurisdiction means that the court is not limited in terms of which types of cases it can hear, including the amount of money in controversy or the parties. Courts of limited jurisdiction are limited as to who is before the court, what type of claim is before the court, and the amount of money in dispute. The New York State court system is diagrammed in the chart. Cases originate in the lower levels (higher numbers) and move up through the system. The highest level in the New York State system is level 1, the Court of Appeals.

Level	Name of New York State Court	Type	Jurisdiction
1st	New York Court of Appeals	Appeals	Limited
2nd	NewYork Appellate Division	Appeals	Limited
3rd	New York Supreme Court	Trial	General
4th	City and local courts	Trial	Limited

Let's take a case that might occur in a New York hotel and follow it through the courts. Suppose a child slips and falls on a room-service tray left in one of the hotel's corridors. The child suffers serious permanent injury to her feet. Her family (the Smiths) sues the hotel, the Imperial. The Smiths are the plaintiffs, the parties bringing the civil lawsuit, and the Imperial is the defendant. This is a civil action for money, not a criminal action, since the Smiths are suing under the theory of negligence, rather than pressing charges. Suppose the Smiths sue for $25,000.

If the Smiths begin in the fourth tier of the New York State court system, their lawsuit will be limited in terms of money to an award of less than either $6000 or $10,000 depending on which court of limited jurisdiction they choose. Since they do not want to be limited to this small a recovery, they will most likely begin in the third tier, before the New York Supreme Court, the court of general jurisdiction, where there is no limit on the amount of money they can recover.

In the Supreme Court, the Smiths will have a trial. If they win, the Imperial Hotel can then appeal to the New York Appellate Division, which hears appeals from the New York Supreme Court. The hotel is then called the appellant, and the Smiths are the appellees. If the Imperial loses at this level, it can choose to appeal again to the New York Court of Appeals, the highest court in New York State. This court hears select cases, and if it refuses to hear the Imperial's appeal, the case is over, or *res judicata* ("a thing decided"). *Res judicata* means that the case of *Smith v. The Imperial Hotel* cannot be heard again, no matter how disappointed either of the parties may be.

There is a distinction between the trial court and the appeals court. In a trial, evidence is presented through witnesses, a trial record is compiled, and a jury or judge renders a verdict. In an appeal, the court reviews the trial record, but it does not hear testimony. Instead the attorneys representing the two parties argue legal "mistakes" that took place at the trial level. The appeals court can reverse the trial court, uphold the trial court, or send the case back down to the trial court for further review. As you read the cases in the textbook, re-member that these cases involve real people—people who had a trial and who are now appealing their case to a higher court.

In summary, subject-matter jurisdiction is the power of the court to hear the case. In New York, the bottom tier is composed of courts of limited jurisdiction. These include courts usually limited in terms of the amount of money that can be awarded, such as a small claims court, or limited in terms of the type of cases they can hear. For example, the small claims court cannot hear matters regarding divorce or custody of children. The court with the broadest power is the New York Supreme Court, and this is where you will most likely litigate large, civil lawsuits. The New York Supreme Court, on the third tier, is not limited as to who the litigants are, the amount in controversy, or the type of claim.

THE FEDERAL COURT SYSTEM

The federal courts operate separately and independently from the fifty state court systems. The first question you may have is, Why have a federal system? Why not litigate all matters in state courts? The answer is that some controversies involve citizens from different states or a federal question. A case can be heard in a federal court for either of the following reasons.

1. Diversity plus $50,000 (diversity of citizenship). If all the plaintiffs are from different states than all the defendants *and* the amount in controversy is greater than $50,000, the federal court has diversity jurisdiction. For example, if the plaintiff is from Virginia and the defendant is from New York and the plaintiff is suing for $50,000, the case can be heard in a federal court. We say the federal courts have subject-matter jurisdiction.

2. Federal-question jurisdiction. If the controversy involves a constitutional question or a patent, copyright, or bankruptcy, the federal courts have subject-matter jurisdiction. There is no minimum required amount of money in a federal-question dispute.

Let's return to the lawsuit between the Smiths and the Imperial Hotel. Can the case be heard in a federal court? Even if the Smiths are from New York and the Imperial is in Massachusetts, the amount in controversy is only $25,000. Therefore, the case could not get into federal court under "diversity plus $50,000." In addition, a slip-and-fall case is not a federal question arising under the Constitution. Under either theory, the case is not eligible for federal court review.

If the Smiths sued for $50,000, however, they could sue in federal court because they would then have met the requirement under diversity plus $50,000. Note that to get into federal court a plaintiff needs to satisfy *either* requirement 1 or 2, not both. Furthermore, the fact that a plaintiff is eligible to go to federal court does not mean that he or she must choose to do so; the plaintiff may still choose to go to state court.

What does the federal system look like? And in what court would the Smiths begin? The chart illustrates the federal court system.

Level	Name of Federal Court	Type	Jurisdiction
1st	U.S. Supreme Court	Appeals	Limited
2nd	U.S. Court of Appeals for the _____ Circuit	Appeals	Limited
3rd	U.S. District Court	Trial	Limited

The Smiths could begin the suit in the U.S. District Court in New York State. This is a trial court, but, again, the subject-matter jurisdiction is limited to either a federal question or diversity plus $50,000. If the Smiths lost in this trial court, they could appeal to the U.S. Court of Appeals for the Second Circuit.

You will notice that the highest court in the federal system is the U.S. Supreme Court. Actually, an appellant may appeal to this court from either the state or federal system. The U.S. Supreme Court agrees to hear about 6–10 percent of all requests each year. Usually, the type of case it decides to hear involves an important legal issue. Our example case may be important to the Smiths and the Imperial Hotel, but it is highly unlikely that the U.S. Supreme Court would find it worthy of review. If the Supreme Court decided not to hear the case, it would be *res judicata* after it was heard by the U.S. Court of Appeals.

In Personam Jurisdiction

The subject-matter jurisdiction of the case is just one factor involved in the decision about where to bring a lawsuit. Once the plaintiff establishes what court is proper in terms of the subject-matter jurisdiction, he or she must next give consideration to *in personam* jurisdiction.

In personam jurisdiction is the power of a particular court over the defendant. We will consider this jurisdiction in the context of the state system rather than the federal system. Suppose the Imperial Hotel is located in Boston. The Smiths are from New York City, and they wish to sue the hotel in New York State. We know that New York's Supreme Court has subject-matter jurisdiction, because that court has general jurisdiction. In order to have *in personam* jurisdiction, a state (in our example, New York State) must have one or more minimal contacts with the defendant. Usually, minimal contacts consist of the defendant's (1) being physically present in the state, (2) having a home in the state, (3) committing a tort in the state, or (4) being a registered corporation in the state. None of these minimal contacts are present in New York in our example: the Imperial Hotel is not present in New York, has not committed a tort in New York, and is not incorporated in New York.

Can the Smiths sue the Imperial in Massachusetts? Does Massachusetts have minimal contacts with the Imperial Hotel? The answer is yes: (1) the hotel is physically present in Massachusetts; (2) the hotel allegedly committed a tort in Massachusetts; (3) the hotel is a corporation incorporated in Massachusetts. Any one of these is sufficient to meet the minimal contacts requirement. Therefore, Massachusetts has *in personam* jurisdiction and a suit can be brought there, but not in New York. Remember that the plaintiffs need both subject-matter jurisdiction and *in personam* jurisdiction to successfully sue the defendant.

Steps in a Civil Lawsuit

This section briefly outlines the basic sequence of steps in a civil lawsuit. The purpose of this section is to familiarize you with civil litigation so that you will be able to deal more constructively with your legal counsel.

Step 1. Plaintiff Identifies the Cause of Action

The first item to be determined is whether a legal cause of action exists. Someone who has been wronged may be hurt or angry, but unless there is some legally recognized cause of action, suing will be a waste of time and money.

Step 2. Plaintiff Decides Appropriate Jurisdiction

If a cause of action exists, the plaintiff must next decide which court has both *in personam* and subject-matter jurisdiction.

Step 3. Plaintiff Files a Complaint

The plaintiff next files papers setting out the cause of action and basically describing what happened and why the lawsuit is being brought. This paper (the complaint) is often accompanied by a summons.

Step 4. Defendant Responds

After the defendant receives the complaint, the defendant has several options. If the defendant does nothing, the plaintiff may proceed and get a judgment against the defendant. This is called a default judgment. The defendant may allow this to occur if he or she has no assets.

The defendant may file an answer. This is a set of papers that respond to every allegation in the plaintiff's complaint. As a general rule, all allegations contained in the complaint that are not denied in the answer are admitted as true. It is important that the defendant answer each allegation, so as not to be liable for simply failing to deny an allegation.

The defendant may also counterclaim in the answer. This means that the defendant is suing the plaintiff in the same lawsuit for a cause of action arising out of the same incident. The defendant may also file motions to dismiss or raise other defenses against the lawsuit.

Step 5. Discovery

Both parties next undertake discovery. Usually, this takes two forms: interrogatories and depositions. Interrogatories are extensive written questions that must be answered in writing under oath. Depositions are testimony given in an actual hearing, which is subsequently transcribed. Although a judge is not present for the taking of depositions, the procedure is similar to a trial in that both attorneys are present and question witnesses and parties under oath. Much information may be gathered before a trial as the result of these procedures.

Step 6. The Trial

After the time for discovery has passed, the parties may settle out of court or actually go to trial. If they go to trial, both sides present evidence through witnesses, a written record of the proceedings is created, and a judge or jury renders a decision or verdict.

Review Questions for Chapter 2

1. What power of the court does subject-matter jurisdiction refer to?

2. What power of the court does *in personam* jurisdiction refer to?

3. Which of the following cases *could* be heard in federal court? Give your reasons why the case could or could not be heard.
   a. A hits B. B sues for $5000.
   b. A, a resident of Vermont, sues B, a resident of New York, and C, a resident of Virginia.

4. A sues B for violating the commerce clause of the U.S. Constitution.

5. A, a resident of New York, sues B, a resident of Pennsylvania, for $50,000.

6. A seeks a divorce from B.

7. A sues B for copyright infringement.

8. Cleaver, a salesperson located in Ohio, brings a vacuum cleaner to Ithaca, New York, and sells the vacuum to Sally Student

for $150. Cleaver returns to Ohio. The vacuum blows up. Sally suffers over $100,000 in personal injuries. Sally wishes to sue Cleaver.

   a. Discuss the subject-matter jurisdiction of the case. (Remember to discuss all possibilities.)

   b. Discuss the *in personam* jurisdiction of the case. (Remember to discuss all possibilities.)

9. What is a cause of action?

10. In your own words, make up a story that includes a plausible, legal cause of action. Make sure you name all the people in the story and identify the plaintiff, defendant, and each person's state of residence.

   a. List *all* the courts that have subject-matter jurisdiction in the case.

   b. Tell which courts having subject-matter jurisdiction also have *in personam* jurisdiction and why.

11. List five options available to a defendant after receiving a summons and complaint and describe the effect of each.

12. Who is present at interrogatories and what occurs?

13. Who is present at depositions and what occurs?

14. List the steps, from selecting a jury to the appeal, that occur in a civil trial.

15. To what court would you bring an appeal?

16. What is the party who appeals a case called? What is the opposing party called?

17. What papers must be prepared to appeal?

18. Describe how an appeal differs from a trial.

CHAPTER 3

The History and Nature of Inns
and the Innkeeper's
Public Duty at Common Law

Historical Development of the Business of Innkeeping

I.   Rules regarding innkeepers are from early English law (1:6).
    A. Innkeepers are engaged in a "public business" (2:2).
    B. As a result, the law holds innkeepers to a legal duty to:
      1. Supply travelers with food and shelter (3:8).
      2. Provide sufficient protection to those he or she accommodates (3:8).
      3. Accept all who apply for lodging (3:1).

The Nature and Definition of an Inn and Other Places of Public Accommodation

I.   "Public" nature of the inn.
    A. An innkeeper has a duty to serve the public (2:1–2:2).
    B. Guests are transient, not permanent (2:4).
    C. To be a common-law inn, an inn must have facilities to provide guests with food (2:5).
II.   Innkeeper not a host for hire (2:3).
    A. The innkeeper holds himself or herself to the public as a party

[22]

willing to accommodate, whereas a host for hire is not engaged in the "regular business of accommodating the public."

III. Definition of an innkeeper and an inn (2:6).

    A. An innkeeper is "the person who on his own account carries on the business of an inn" (textbook, p. 15).

    B. "An inn is a house where all who conduct themselves properly, and who are able and ready to pay for their entertainment, are received, if there is accommodation for them, and who, without any stipulated engagement as to the duration of their stay, or as to the rate of compensation are, while there, supplied at a reasonable charge with their meals, their lodging, and such services and attention as are necessarily incident to the use of the house as a temporary home." *Cromwell v. Stephens* (textbook, p. 20).

    C. Motels, hotels, and inns are generally the same. Legal distinctions exist by statute in the areas of zoning, building, alcohol control, and advertising (2:9).

IV. Lodging facilities are *not* inns (2:11–2:15).

    A. Apartment hotels, rooming houses, boardinghouses, lodging-houses, apartment houses, and bed-and-breakfast establishments are not inns.

    B. In New York State, whether a building provides services to its tenants was an important consideration for determining whether the building was a hotel or a rooming house. *Whitehall Hotel v. Gaynor* (textbook, pp. 20–23). The court discussed the definition of a hotel under New York's Metropolitan Hotel Industry Stabilization Code noting that the code was amended to include the phrase "provides hotel services" as part of the definition of a hotel.

    C. A YMCA that admitted all who applied for accommodation was not limited to "members only" and therefore was considered to be the same as a hotel or an inn. *YMCA of Greater New York McBurney Branch v. Plotkin* (textbook, p. 24).

V. Taxes on municipal hotel room use and occupancy.

    A. A city tax on lodgers was held to be illegal in *Montana Inn-*

keepers Ass'n v. City of Billings (textbook, p. 25) because only the state could impose a tax on services, and use of a hotel room is a service, not goods.

B. A city tax on lodgers was held to be legal in *Springfield Hotel-Motel Ass'n v. City of Springfield* (textbook, p. 25) because in Illinois cities are given the power to make rules about tangible goods, and a hotel room is a tangible good in Illinois.

C. In *Leventhol v. City of Philadelphia* (textbook, pp. 26–30), Philadelphia's hotel room rental tax was held to be legal.

VI. Restaurants (2:16).

A. Restaurants are not inns, and generally there is no public duty of accommodation. (See also 15:1.)

VII. Common carriers (2:17).

A. Common carriers furnish transportation to the public (airplanes, buses, cargo carriers). They have a higher standard of law than private carriers and are regulated by statute.

The Innkeeper's Public Duty at Common Law

I. An innkeeper has a public calling (3:1–3:2) and a fundamental duty to the public to:

A. Admit all who apply (3:3).

B. Provide adequate service (3:8).

C. Serve the public equally without discrimination (3:9).

D. Charge only a reasonable price (3:10).

II. Duty to admit travelers (3:3).

A. A "traveler" is not only a person engaged in a journey, but anyone who calls at the inn for admission (subject to lawful reasons not to admit), even at night (3:4, 3:6).

B. Duty extends to minors and other travelers incapable of making binding contracts for necessaries (3:5). (For a discussion of minors and necessaries see Chapter 6, Capacity.)

C. Failure to accommodate may be a misdemeanor (3:7).
III. Duty to shelter and entertain guests (3:8).
IV. Duty not to discriminate (3:9). (For a detailed discussion of this duty see Chapters 4 and 5 and textbook, Chapter 4.)
  A. Common law imposes a duty on innkeepers to refrain from discrimination.
  B. Federal and state statutes prohibit discrimination in inns and other places of public accommodation.
V. Duty to make reasonable charges for services (3:10). (For a detailed discussion of this duty see Chapter 23 and textbook, Chapter 21.)

Review Questions for Chapter 3 and Textbook, Chapters 1–3

1. What is the difference between an inn and a boardinghouse?
2. What is the significance of distinguishing an inn from other types of establishments?
3. What is the source of U.S. hotel law?
4. You are in charge of the front desk of the Fabulous Hotel, located in Wichita, Kansas. One evening the following people appear, seeking admittance. State the rule for why you would or would not have to answer your public calling.
  a. An intoxicated adult. ✗
  b. A minor, aged 17, and his girlfriend, aged 16. ✓
  c. A resident of Wichita, Kansas, not traveling anywhere. ✓
  d. An adult arriving at 4 A.M. ✓

1. An inn is a public place where transient guests are received for accommodation.

2. Legal distinctions exist by statute in the areas of zoning, building, alcohol control, and advertising.

CHAPTER 4

Introduction to Constitutional Law

This chapter introduces concepts that are fundamental to all areas of U.S. law. Because all U.S. laws, whether formulated by judges or legislatures, must meet the minimum standard articulated in the Constitution, it is not possible to study any U.S. law without first understanding basic tenets of the U.S. Constitution. This chapter discusses components of the Constitution that are especially relevant to business transactions. It also lays a foundation for contracts, torts, and property and discrimination law, which are discussed in subsequent chapters.

Before you begin this chapter look at the text of the Constitution in the Appendix. As we consider each of the relevant constitutional provisions, you will find it helpful to read the full text of the provision as it appears in the Constitution.

The Supreme Law of the Land

As a theoretical starting point, consider the phrase, "The United States Constitution is the Supreme Law of the Land." That means that all laws passed by Congress (the federal legislative body) and all laws passed by state legislatures, as well as laws "made" by judges and administrative agencies must meet constitutional standards.

Suppose that state X passes a law imposing a tax on all hotel patrons. Management of the hotel is worried that this particular tax will have a deleterious effect on the hotel's ability to attract guests. As a result, the Fabulous Hotel challenges the constitutionality of the law. It may argue, for example, that the tax violates the "taxing power of the Constitution." If the courts ultimately decide that the law is in fact unconstitutional, the tax may no longer be imposed on hotel guests.

Unconstitutional laws remain in effect until they are challenged, and legislatures do pass unconstitutional laws. Until it is challenged and reviewed by the courts, a law's constitutionality may indeed be in question. Can you think of laws that in your lifetime have been declared unconstitutional by the U.S. Supreme Court?

Powers Reserved to the States

It is helpful to consider the historical context in which the U.S. Constitution was written. The Founding Fathers were escaping a government ruled by a king and replete with religious persecution. When they wrote the Constitution, one of their primary goals was to decentralize the federal government. This was accomplished in part by the Tenth Amendment, which states, "The powers not delegated to the United States by the Constitution . . . are reserved to the States."

That means that if the Constitution does not explicitly state that the power is given (enumerated) to the federal government, then the power is "given" to the individual states (reserved powers). Note that Article 1, Section 8 sets out Congress's enumerated powers. These are the power to tax, borrow money, regulate interstate commerce, regulate bankruptcy, constitute the federal court system, and declare war. Of course there are many powers not contained in this list. Those powers not specifically set out are delegated to the states to regulate and monitor. But if a state legislature passes a law that is specifically enumerated to the federal government, that law should be held unconstitutional.

Applicability of the Constitution to the Hospitality Industry

Once you are a manager in the hotel industry, you may find many situations in which the Constitution has special relevance to your work. These areas include the regulation of the sale of food and beverages, taxes, interstate commerce, and forms of discrimination, to name a few.

As you study some of the individual components of the Constitution, keep in mind that many of these provisions have been used in litigation involving hotels and restaurants. Consider what the litigants could have done differently to prevent such lawsuits.

THE COMMERCE CLAUSE (ARTICLE I, SECTION 8)

"The Congress shall have Power . . . To regulate Commerce with foreign Nations, and among the several States, and with the Indian Tribes."

Article 1, Section 8 sets out the powers specifically enumerated to the federal government. The provision dealing with commerce is called the commerce clause.

The commerce clause has many ramifications that to a large extent exceed the scope of this brief discussion. From a historical viewpoint you could study a tremendous amount of precedent involving this one provision of the Constitution. After all, the courts have examined this clause for almost two hundred years. Fortunately, as a result of this scrutiny, some general conclusions may be drawn about the application of the commerce clause to businesses.

First, the Constitution specifically delegates the power to regulate commerce between the states to Congress, not to the states. Commerce between states is called interstate commerce. Not only must the commerce be interstate for Congress to regulate it, but the law must have some rational basis. Suppose, for example, that the federal government passes a law that all hotels must have specially modified entrances to accommodate guests in wheelchairs. Assume that the hotels are engaged in interstate commerce; that is, their business crosses state lines. The question you should consider is whether Congress has the power to make a law that will have an impact on a private business. The general conclusion, based on historical court decisions, is this: the courts will uphold any law that Congress passes that has a "rational basis" in its commerce power. A rational basis means that the law does not unduly interfere with interstate commerce, yet promotes a worthwhile purpose—in this case, accommodation of the handicapped. In effect, the commerce clause acts as a bridge between federal laws and private conduct. In this example, the commerce clause gives Congress the power to make the law, since restrictions on people's ability to travel affect interstate commerce.

Examples of cases involving the commerce clause follow.

Commerce with Foreign Nations

Japan Lines, Ltd., a Japanese corporation, shipped containers to California, where they remained for approximately three weeks while undergoing repairs and awaiting loading to another port. All the containers were taxed in Japan. California imposed an *ad valorem* tax (a tax based on a percentage of the value of the property) on Japan Lines, Ltd. by assessing the number of containers that were "fairly representative" by their "average presence" in the taxing county throughout the whole year. Does the state of California have the power to regulate commerce with a foreign country's businesses?

In ruling on *Japan Lines, Ltd. v. Los Angeles*, 441 U.S. 434 (1979), the U.S. Supreme Court held that "multiple taxation is offensive to the Commerce Clause. . . ." A state tax in the instrumentalities of foreign commerce may impair federal uniformity in an area where federal uniformity is essential. Foreign commerce is preeminently a matter of national concern. California prevents this nation from "speaking with one voice" in the regulation of foreign trade.

The action by California was held to be unconstitutional.

You can draw two important conclusions from this case. First, California's attempt to regulate an area that the Constitution specifically enumerates to the federal branch was ruled unconstitutional. Second, note the "rational basis"; it makes sense for only one entity to be taxing foreign governments. Allowing individual states to tax every entity within their borders would "impair uniformity and severely impair commerce." After all, what foreign entity would want to do business in the United States if every state it entered had the power to tax it?

Commerce between States

As mentioned above, the commerce clause gives Congress the power to regulate commerce between states (interstate commerce). Once commerce crosses state lines, it comes under federal purview.

If state X passes a law pertaining to commerce within its own borders, however, that is *intra*state commerce. As a general rule, only states, and not the federal government, may regulate such activity. Sometimes, however, intrastate activity *is* regulated by the federal government. This occurs when intrastate activity affects interstate commerce (the affectation doctrine). The *Heart of Atlanta Motel*, *Katzenbach*, and *Wickard* cases, described below, are examples of the affectation doctrine.

The owner of a motel located in Atlanta, Georgia, refused to rent rooms to blacks. At the time, Georgia had no laws outlawing discrimination against blacks at hotels. However, there was in existence a federal law—the Civil Rights Act of 1964, Title II—that prohibited discrimination in any "inn, hotel, motel, restaurant, or motion picture house if it affects commerce." The motel was located on a major interstate highway and had billboards on that highway that attracted interstate travelers. The motel also advertised in magazines having a national circulation. Can Congress pass a law regulating the activity of a private motel in a single state when that activity affects interstate commerce?

In ruling on *Heart of Atlanta Motel, Inc. v. United States* (textbook, p. 68) the U.S. Supreme Court said that even if the activity was deemed to be "local in character" nevertheless interstate commerce feels the pinch. "It does not matter how local the operation which applies the squeeze." The Act of 1964 is based on the power of Congress to "regulate commerce between the states, and the power to make all laws necessary and proper for carrying into effect the powers vested in the Congress by the Constitution." The use of the commerce clause as the legal basis for the Act permits regulation of individual activities without the need for finding state action. Generally, a place of public accommodation comes within the meaning of the Act if its operations affect interstate commerce. In particular a lodging establishment is included if it serves transient guests and a restaurant is included if it serves interstate travelers or if a substantial portion of the food it serves has moved in commerce.

Thus, activity that is purely intrastate but affects commerce (precluding blacks from freely moving in commerce) "becomes" interstate commerce, making the private action subject to federal laws.

In a related case, *Katzenbach v. McClung* (textbook, pp. 55, 69) Ollie's Barbecue refused to serve blacks. This restaurant was located eleven miles from the local interstate highway. The owner of the restaurant claimed that he was engaged in local business. He challenged the provision of Title II of the Civil Rights Act that holds that a restaurant affects interstate commerce if a substantial portion of the food it serves has moved through interstate commerce even though the restaurant does not serve interstate travelers. The activity of Ollie's Barbecue seemingly had no direct effect on interstate commerce, as there was no evidence that interstate travelers were customers. The court reasoned, however, that since exclusion of blacks caused the restaurant to serve fewer customers, the restaurant could buy less food through interstate commerce. Thus Ollie's, seemingly a local business, was deemed to be engaged in interstate commerce, and Title II's nondiscrimination provisions applied.

Another extreme example of intrastate commerce becoming interstate is the case of *Wickard v. Filburn*, 317 U.S. 111 (1942). An Ohio farmer objected to the application of the Agricultural Adjustment Act, a federal law, to his business, a local farm that grew wheat for home consumption. Nevertheless, the Supreme Court held that even wheat grown for home consumption affects interstate commerce. Their rationale was that the *aggregate* of all homegrown wheat has an effect on the price and market conditions of wheat everywhere. Thus, the aggregate of individual farmers had an impact on interstate commerce.

These cases are important to remember when studying textbook Chapter 4, which deals specifically with discrimination. The commerce clause is a fundamental theoretical basis upon which federal laws become applicable to seemingly private intrastate activity. Without this basis, it would be necessary to find other constitutional provisions to connect local activity and federal legislation.

The Supremacy Clause (Article VI)

"This Constitution, and the Laws of the United States . . . ; and all Treaties made, . . . under the Authority of the United States, shall be the supreme Law of the Land."

The provision in Article VI that designates the Constitution as the supreme law of the land is known as the supremacy clause. When Congress passes a law that directly conflicts with a state law, the state law may be challenged as a violation of the supremacy clause. In general, when there is a conflict between federal and state law, the federal law will prevail, or preempt the state law. This is called the preemption doctrine.

Suppose Congress passes a law that states, "Airline liability for passengers on airplanes is limited to $50,000." Suppose also that the state of Pennsylvania passes a law that states, "Airline liability for passengers shall have no monetary limits." Obviously there is a direct conflict between the state law and the federal law. Which law prevails? In general, preemption means that the federal law has precedence when:

1. Congressional intent was to supersede other laws. This is known as express preemption—that is, Congress expressly stated that its purpose in passing the law was to preempt other laws. Usually such intent is manifested in the *Congressional Record*, which contains comments about the purpose of legislation from the sponsors.
2. The laws cannot peacefully coexist. This is known as inferred preemption. Peaceful coexistence means that the two laws may stand side by side, without being incompatible. For example, if Pennsylvania's law stated that airline liability is limited to $50,000, but to recover damages, passengers need to fill out a particular form, one could argue that both laws can exist at the same time; they are not in conflict. Thus, preemption would not take place.

THE BILL OF RIGHTS

The first ten amendments to the constitution are commonly called the Bill of Rights. The three amendments you will study here are

> First—freedom of speech and religion.
> Fourth—freedom from unreasonable searches and seizures.
> Fifth—protection against self-incrimination.

The First Amendment

"Congress shall make no law . . . abridging the freedom of speech . . . or the right of the people peaceably to assemble."

In the hospitality industry, First Amendment issues may arise in many contexts. For example, do protesters have the right to gather in the lobby? Must the hotel allow distribution of leaflets in the hotel? Outside on the sidewalk? Is advertising by the hotel commercial speech?

Remember, an inn is a place of public accommodation and innkeepers have a duty to accommodate the public. Because they serve the general public, inns may not lawfully exclude without justification. While the First Amendment does guarantee free speech and the right to assemble, it does not make such a guarantee if, in the confines of a hotel or restaurant, speech or assembly causes a disturbance, damages property, injures others, or otherwise disrupts the business.

At other places of business, such as shopping malls, the courts have considered First Amendment rights in some detail. For example, in *Shad v. Smith Haven Mall* (textbook, pp. 48–49), the New York courts held that a private shopping mall may curtail First Amendment rights by prohibiting leafleting on the premises. But once the mall makes itself accessible to the public for any kind of noncommercial expression, it then has a duty not to discriminate.

Another issue in the scope of First Amendment rights concerns commercial speech, or speech emanating from a business rather than in a personal context. Commercial speech is not as protected as personal speech. Several cases in the hotel industry deal with forms of advertising. May a state pass a law regulating the manner in which a motel advertises its rates? The answer is yes. In *State of Arizona v. Hutchinson*, 699 P.2d 402 (1985), an Arizona motel posted an outdoor advertising sign that read:

$14—Single
Free HBO—Phones
U-Haul Parking

An Arizona statute required that motel owners post both the minimum and the maximum rates for their rooms. The motel owner objected on the ground that the advertisement was free speech and therefore was protected. The court stated that "states retain the authority to regulate advertising that is inherently misleading . . . [but they must do so] with care and in a manner no more extensive than reasonably necessary to further substantial material interests." Thus the state did not violate the innkeeper's First Amendment rights since the advertising was deceptive.

The Fourth Amendment

"... the people [shall] ... be secure ... in their ... houses ... against unreasonable searches and seizures."

As a basic premise, the police must have "probable cause"—that is, evidence that a crime has likely taken place (or is about to take place)—before they may search premises or seize contraband. If the police have information from an informant, they will often seek a warrant from a magistrate that allows them to search premises or seize contraband. If a crime is committed in the presence of police, they have probable cause without seeking a warrant and can immediately react by searching or seizing or both.

What then is an *unreasonable* search and seizure? In general, it is one without probable cause or one for which there is no statutory basis. Many states, for instance, have laws that permit searches without a warrant. For example, in Florida, the hotel commission has the right to enter a hotel without a search warrant and inspect the premises for possible gambling operations (*In re Smith*, 74 So. 2d 353). Most states have provisions that allow health officials to inspect without warrants. Such a provision would include areas that process food and beverages. All states have laws that require innkeepers to maintain a registry of their guests subject at all times to inspection by a federal peace officer.

In the absence of a particular statute or probable cause, however, both the innkeeper and the innkeeper's guests have a reasonable expectation of privacy. Thus, a guest may reasonably expect that telephone calls from his room are recorded by the hotel for billing purposes only and that a record of his calls may not be transmitted to others without legal process (*People v. Blair*; textbook, pp. 205–6). Yet, when the management believes that illegal activity is taking place, it may infringe on a guest's privacy. In *People v. Soles* (textbook, pp. 206–7) the California courts held that a motel manager's act in staying on the guest's telephone line and electronically eavesdropping was permissible "to the extent necessary to carry out the protective search."

Similarly, although the innkeeper may not consent to an inspection of a guest's room without the guest's permission, after the rental period has expired, a guest's reasonable expectations of privacy are "greatly diminished" with respect to the right of motel management to enter (*Sumdum v. State*; textbook, pp. 199–200).

And in *Berger v. State*, 257 S.E.2d 8 (Ga. App., 1979), hotel management personnel opened unlocked items found on the premises to determine ownership so that they could return lost or misplaced property to its proper owner. This action was held to be an authorized search, not a violation of the Fourth Amendment.

The Fifth Amendment

"No person . . . shall be compelled in any criminal case to be a witness against himself."

Most likely, you have heard the Fifth Amendment referred to as "the right not to testify against yourself." In a business context, this amendment has implications with regard to turning over records of a business as well as to testifying in a criminal trial against oneself. As a general rule, this amendment protects an individual from self-incrimination. *Individual* in this context means a person or a business run as a sole proprietorship.

The Fifth Amendment does not, however, protect a corporation. If the Fabulous Hotel, Inc. receives a subpoena to turn over all its tax records for the previous six years, this amendment will not protect the hotel; the records must be turned over. Similarly, the amendment does not protect the records of a partnership.

Summary of constitutional law concepts

Concept	Explanation

Commerce clause	Congress regulates commerce:
	    Between states
	    Between states and foreign nations
	    If local activity affects interstate activity (affectation doctrine)
	    State law regulates purely local (intrastate) activity.

Supremacy clause	When federal and state laws conflict, federal law prevails over state law if:
	    Congress intended it to (express preemption)
	    The two laws cannot peacefully coexist (inferred preemption)

First Amendment	Guarantees freedom of speech and assembly. Limited in hotels if activity disturbs or disrupts. Commercial speech not "as protected" as personal speech. State may limit if deceptive.
Fourth Amendment	Warrantless searches are prohibited, but warrantless food, health, and safety searches are allowed.
Fifth amendment	Protects individuals and sole proprietorships from self-incrimination; does not protect corporations and partnerships.

Review Questions for Chapter 4

Your answers to the following questions should be based on rules and cases, not on opinion or facts.

1. A guest of the Fabulous Hotel calls down to the front desk to report unusual activity in the next room, Room 111. As a result of that call the following events take place. Discuss each one in the context of the Fourth Amendment.
   a. The night manager bangs on the door of Room 111, receives no response, and then enters the room.
   b. The manager listens outside the room to conversations taking place within the room.
   c. The manager, accompanied by the police, enters the room. The police have a valid search warrant.
   d. The manager calls the police. They enter the room without the manager and without a search warrant.

2. A pizza house located in Small Town, New York, refuses to serve African Americans or women. The pizza house is not located near any interstate highway and serves only local clientele.
   a. On the basis of *Katzenbach v. McClung*, is the pizza house subject to Title II?
   b. If so, under what theory?
   c. What ramifications follow when Title II applies?
   d. Does the policy enunciated by the court in *Wickard v. Filburn* apply?

3. In what type of activities could a business engage that would make it purely an intrastate enterprise?

4. The U.S. Supreme Court is the "supreme law of the land." State A passes a law requiring that all restaurants within state borders limit their outside signs to dimensions of 6 feet by 6 feet. There is no federal law conflicting with this state law. As CEO of the restaurant, you object to that limitation. What constitutional basis would your attorneys have to challenge the state statute? Discuss their argument.

C H A P T E R 5

Discrimination in Places of Public Accommodation: Civil Rights

I.   Overview (4:1–4:4).
   A. An innkeeper has a common-law duty to admit all who apply.
       1. Restaurants do not have the same duty (4:2).
       2. Race tracks do not have the same duty. *Arone v. Sullivan County Harness Racing Association, Inc.* (textbook, p. 46).
   B. This common-law rule was not enforced in many regions of the United States.
   C. As a result of discrimination against both guests and employees, both federal and state governments enacted antidiscrimination legislation.
II. Title II of the Civil Rights Act (42 U.S.C.; §2000) (4:4–4:8).
   A. Title II prohibits discrimination on the basis of race, color, religion, or national origin at "any inn, motel or other establishment which provides lodging to transient guests" (4:5). (For restaurants, see E, below.) Title II does *not* prohibit discrimination on the basis of age, sex, physical ability, or sexual orientation.
   B. There must be a connection between the private activity and the federal government. The commerce clause is one way the federal government can apply its antidiscrimination laws to private activity.
       1. In *Daniel v. Paul*, 395 U.S. 298 (U.S. Supreme Court,

[39]

1969) the U.S. Supreme Court held that the Little Nixon Club, an amusement park in Arkansas, was a "place of amusement" subject to the antidiscrimination requirements of Title II. The court said that "it is a covered public accommodation if it serves or offers to serve interstate travelers, or a substantial portion of the food it serves has moved in interstate commerce." Because the owners advertised with the intent to attract interstate travelers, the court concluded that the Little Nixon Club offered to serve out-of-state travelers, thus making it subject to Title II.

C. Examples of accommodations subject to Title II.
1. A beach apartment that offers lodging for transient guests by the week.
2. A YMCA with a dormitory facility.
3. A trailer park that provides lodging to transient guests.
4. A health club, swimming pool, or gym operated by a hotel or motel and considered part of the facility.

D. Establishments that are *not* covered.
1. Those that are purely local: no commerce clause or state action involved.
2. Mrs. Murphy's Boardinghouse: serving five or fewer lodgers and occupied also by the owner.
3. Bars, lounges, nightclubs, bowling alleys, golf courses *if* they:
   a) Do not serve food moving through interstate commerce.
   b) Do not offer entertainment moving through interstate commerce.
4. Private clubs (4:5). Factors the courts will consider (textbook, pp. 56–57).
   a) The selectiveness of the group in the admission of members.
   b) The existence of formal membership procedures.
   c) The degree of membership control over internal governance, especially membership selection.

    d) The history and purpose of the organization (e.g., was it created to avoid civil rights legislation?).

    e) The use of club facilities by nonmembers.

    f) The substantiality of dues.

    g) Whether the organization advertises.

    h) The predominance of profit motive.

E. Restaurants (4:5).

  1. Title II prohibits discrimination in any "restaurant, cafeteria, lunchroom, lunch counter, soda fountain, or other facility principally engaged in selling food for consumption on the premises."

  2. Even if the business's product is not primarily food, the court may find that Title II applies if a substantial part of its goods are moved in interstate commerce. This even includes the syrup used to make a soft drink.

  3. Summary of Title II's application to restaurants.

    a) The establishment is principally engaged in selling food.

    b) The food is fit for consumption on the premises.

    c) The restaurant serves interstate travelers.

    d) A substantial portion of the food moves in interstate commerce.

    e) Or, state action is present; that is, a federal or state interest results in federal law applying to seemingly private activity, such as a state license.

III. Additional federal protection.

A. In 1866, Congress passed 42 U.S.C.A. sections 1981–1985 to protect blacks from discrimination. Relatively dormant until the 1960s these statutes were "discovered" by civil rights litigators.

B. 42 U.S.C.A. section 1981 provides for all U.S. citizens "the same right to make and enforce contracts . . . as is enjoyed by white citizens."

C. 42 U.S.C.A. section 1982 provides that all U.S. citizens have "the same rights as those enjoyed by white citizens, to purchase, lease and hold real and personal property."

      D. Both section 1981 and section 1982 were used in *Durham v. Red Lake Fishing and Hunting Club*, 666 F. Supp. 954 (1987). An African American applied for and was denied membership to the club. The club defended its action on the ground that it was private and therefore not subject to Title II. In addition, the club argued that the private club exemption was applicable to sections 1981 and 1982. The court held that the plaintiff was discriminated against on the basis of race and that both statutes were applicable.

      E. Likewise, *Hernandez v. Erlenbusch*, 368 F. Supp. 752 (D. Or. 1973), was brought under 42 U.S.C.A. sections 1981, 1982, and 1985. The court held that buying a beer at a bar constituted the purchase of personal property as well as the making of a contract. The court stated that "there is no question but that 42 U.S.C.A. sections 1981 and 1982 have been interpreted to ban the discrimination alleged in these cases."

IV. Sex discrimination (4:6).

      A. Not covered by Title II. Look at state statutes for protection against sex discrimination.

      B. In *DeCrow v. Hotel Syracuse Corp.* (textbook, p. 59), which was decided before New York's sex discrimination statute was enacted, the Hotel Syracuse refused to serve a woman a drink at the bar. The court held that Title II does not prohibit such discrimination.

      C. A state license to operate a bar has been held to be state action thus making discrimination against women "unreasonable" under state law. *Seidenberg v. McSorley's Old Ale House, Inc.* (textbook, pp. 59–60).

      D. In *Koire v. Metro Car Wash* (textbook, pp. 81–87), "ladies night" at a bar was held to violate California law as discriminatory.

V. Age discrimination (4:7).

      A. Title II does not prohibit discrimination on the basis of age.

      B. Many states have laws that do, but the ages protected vary. See

Chapter 26 for a discussion of the Age Discrimination in Employment Act (ADEA).

VI. Remedies and penalties for violations of Title II (4:8).

A. Injunctive relief—the government may make the discriminating facility admit the person.

VII. State civil rights laws (4:11–4:25).

A. States have passed additional laws to protect their citizens against forms of discrimination not covered by Title II.

B. The chart summarizes New York State's antidiscrimination laws.

Section of New York civil rights law	Covers:	Applies to:	
§40	All places of public accommodation, including resorts and amusement facilities	Race Creed Color National origin	
§40-c	All places of public accommodation, including resorts and amusement facilities	Sex Marital status Disability	
§44-a	Accommodations or facilities of innkeepers or common carriers	Race Creed Color National origin	Applies to any person, misdemeanor to exclude
Executive Order 296	All places of accommodation, including resorts and amusement facilities	Race Creed Color National origin Sex Marital status Disability	Illegal to withhold accommodations or extension of credit

C. Cases interpreting New York State antidiscrimination laws (4:16).
   1. A restaurant's refusal to serve plaintiff "on purely personal grounds" *not* on the basis of his race, creed, or color was not covered by Title II and therefore plaintiff could not recover under a civil rights violation theory. *Noble v. Higgins* (textbook, p. 72).
   2. A hotel's refusal to admit an interracial couple was held to violate New York Civil Rights Law section 40 in *Hobson v. York Studios, Inc.* (textbook, pp. 73–74).
   3. In *Batavia Lodge v. Division of Human Rights* (textbook, pp. 74–76), the refusal to serve blacks at a Moose Lodge bar was held to be a violation of New York Executive Law, even though the lodge was a private club, because it was being used in a public manner.
VIII. Other forms of discrimination.
   A. Clothing (4:19).
      1. In *Hales v. Ojai Valley Inn and Country Club* (textbook, pp. 77–79), when a brochure stated that men were "requested to wear a tie" at dinner and plaintiff refused to wear one and was excluded from the dining area, he made out a *prima facie* case of misleading advertising and sex discrimination.
      2. In *Renteria v. Dirty Dan's, Inc.* (textbook, pp. 87–90), a bar's refusal to serve a patron because he had a motorcycle insignia on his clothing was held to be discriminatory under California's Unruh Act (prohibits arbitrary discrimination).
   B. Long hair.
      1. In *Braun v. Swiston* (textbook, p. 81), it was held that a male patron who was evicted from a bar because of the length of his hair could sue for sex discrimination because women with long hair were served in the bar.
   C. Marital status, disability, or credit (4:20–4:22).
      1. An establishment may not discriminate because of marital

status, disability, or credit under New York Executive Law
section 296(a).

D. The male-only civic club (4:23).

   1. The national Kiwanis refused to admit females to its clubs.
In *Kiwanis Club of Great Neck, Inc. v. Board of Trustees of
Kiwanis International* (textbook, pp. 91–93), the U.S. Supreme Court stated that because the club is private and there
is no "connection" (state action, or nexus) to federal or state
laws, Kiwanis could discriminate against women by pre-
venting their admission.

   2. In *Roberts v. United States Jaycees* (textbook, pp. 96–103),
the U.S. Supreme Court found the Jaycees' refusal to admit
women discriminatory. The court reasoned that this holding
did not interfere with the Jaycees' First Amendment rights
because the Jaycees is not the sort of association entitled to
this constitutional protection.

Review Questions for Chapter 5 and Textbook, Chapter 4

Your answers to the following questions should be based on rules
and cases, not on opinion or facts.

1. The Fabulous Hotel, located in a major metropolitan area, refuses to allow unaccompanied women to have a drink in its lounge
between the hours of 5 and 7 P.M.

   a. What is the application of Title II to this situation?

   b. Suppose the women denied access argue that a hotel is open to
the public and therefore must admit them for a drink. What is
the validity of that argument?

   c. What is the women's best argument, that is, the one most likely
to succeed in court? What legal basis would you use in their
behalf?

2. Apples and Peaches is an exclusive organization at a prestigious

eastern Ivy League institution. In order to be admitted to A&P, one must be tapped by its members and then go through an induction. To date, the only people selected have been wealthy, white, and male. A lawsuit is brought on behalf of all females, African Americans, and Asian Americans against A&P, on the grounds of discrimination. Discuss the chances of their succeeding in the lawsuit. Make sure that in your discussion you define what constitutes a club.

3. Gerry Gambler has a photographic memory that enables him frequently to beat the odds at gambling tables. His reputation gets around, and the Fabulous Hotel refuses to allow him to gamble on the premises. In fact management has him evicted from the hotel. Gerry sues the hotel for discrimination. On what basis, if any, could he bring a lawsuit? What do you think are his chances for success?

4. What factors determine whether a restaurant is engaged in interstate commerce? What is the significance of being engaged in interstate commerce? Can you think of an example of a restaurant that would be exempt from Title II?

5. Larry Longhair enters the Conservative Restaurant and orders a cheeseburger. The counter help refuse to wait on Larry. Discuss Larry's chances of succeeding in both a state and a federal claim under each of the following circumstances.

    a. A lawsuit based solely on the length of his hair.

    b. A lawsuit based on Larry's claim that he was not waited on because he is a homosexual.

    c. A lawsuit based on the fact that the restaurant evicted him because Larry entered the restaurant barefoot and shirtless.

    d. A lawsuit based on Larry's contention that the waitstaff feared he has AIDS and therefore refused to wait on him.

6. The personnel director of the Fabulous Hotel decides not to hire a prospective employee for the reasons given below. Assume the hotel is located in New York City. Discuss whether the applicants listed in a–e have a meritorious cause of action under New York State anti-discrimination statutes.

a. The applicant does not speak English well.
b. The twenty-three-year-old applicant is too young.
c. The applicant is male.
d. The applicant has a six-month-old child.
e. The applicant is Catholic.

PART II

CONTRACTUAL ASPECTS OF INNKEEPERS, GUESTS, AND OTHERS

C H A P T E R   6

Introduction to Contracts

Chapters 5–8 of the textbook detail the contractual relationship between the innkeeper and others. To understand contractual problems endemic to innkeepers, you first need a general understanding of contract law. This overview of contract law is not meant to take the place of legal advice. Nor will it make you an expert in contract law. What you should derive from these materials is an appreciation of the complexities of contract law and a preventive attitude. Warding off the possibility of a contract lawsuit is a cost-saving measure. Furthermore, you should acquire an understanding of black letter law, that is, the theories of law, in the context of innkeeping and restaurant management contracts. In that context, contracts are the underlying foundation for determining:

- What the relationship is between the innkeeper and another
- Whether someone is a guest of the hotel or is in another category
- When registration takes place, thereby establishing the innkeeper-guest relationship
- What is a reservation—a basic contractual relationship
- What defenses the innkeeper has against enforcement of the contract with guests
- The underlying theory for holding guests liable for payment of charges incurred at the hotel
- The underlying theory for collecting monies owed from guests

'he topics covered in this chapter include the following:

- Determining which law applies—UCC or common law
- The five elements of contract formation
    Offer ✓
    Acceptance ✓
    Consideration ✓
    Capacity ✓
    Legality ✓
- Defenses to contract formation
    Fraud
    Undue influence
    Duress
    Impossibility
- Which contracts must be in writing
    Contracts for the sale of real property
    Contracts for the sale of goods valued at greater than $500
    Contracts that cannot be performed within a year
- Damages and remedies
    Money damages
    Nonmoney damages
    The concept of the duty to mitigate damages

The Laws Governing Contract Formation

Contract law is governed by two bodies of law: the Uniform Commercial Code and the common law. If the contract concerns the sale of goods, it is governed by the Uniform Commercial Code (UCC). The UCC states that goods are "moveable and tangible." All fifty states have adopted the UCC in some form. This means that the rules for commercial contracts and transactions are basically the same throughout the United States.

What is the purpose of the UCC? Imagine that you are a New York State resident who desires to sell goods to a resident of Pennsylvania. What contract rules apply? As a merchant, do you have to consult a lawyer each time you enter into a contract? The purpose of the UCC is to make transactions between people who sell or buy goods—whether merchants or not—subject to the same rules. Obviously, commerce will run more smoothly if the laws are basically the same between the states and when people can sell and buy goods without having to seek legal advice for every transaction.

If the contract is *not* for the sale of goods, it is governed by the common law. Recall from Chapter 1 that the common law consists of judges' decisions. General rules about formation and enforcement of contracts can be drawn from these court decisions. But such judge-made law is not necessarily uniform because it is made by different people in different states at different times.

As a hotelier, you will need to know which body of law applies to a particular contract. For example, warranties apply to goods sold pursuant to the UCC but do not apply to contracts under the common law. When you accept a guest for overnight lodging, you enter into a contract that is governed by principles of common law. Selling food in the restaurant, however, is governed by the UCC. What difference does it make which set of rules applies? In the example just cited, the UCC has a warranty about the quality of goods; the common law does not. A guest could not sue for breach of warranty for the quality of the hotel room, but could for the quality of the food. Many other differences exist; we will study a few throughout this chapter.

- Examples of contracts governed by the Uniform Commercial Code (those that involve goods—"moveable and tangible" items):
    Purchase of food for the hotel's restaurants
    Purchase of linens
    Contract for electricity
- Examples of contracts governed by the common law (those that involve items that are *not* goods—are not tangible or moveable):
    Employment contracts

Insurance contracts
Contract with a company to pave the parking lot (a service)

The Five Elements of a Contract

Once you are a party to a contract, it can be enforced by the courts. So it is important to recognize when you have entered into a contract. If, for example, I tell you that I will give you a ride home from the library, that offer is not a contract, but is more like a gift. As you will learn later, the offer lacks consideration, an essential element of a contract. If you tried to sue me for failing to give you a ride home, your lawsuit would be unsuccessful.

Suppose, however, that you and I enter into a contract for the sale and delivery of crystal stemware to your hotel by 3:00 P.M. tomorrow, and when the time arrives, I refuse to deliver. This promise may well have all the elements of a contract, and my breach may make me liable to you for monetary damages.

For a contract to be legally enforceable, it must have five elements: offer, acceptance, consideration, capacity, and legality. Once you enter into a contract that has all five elements, you incur a legal liability.

FIRST ELEMENT: THE OFFER

The two parties to a contract are the offeror and the offeree. Suppose an offeror says, "I will sell you a basset hound puppy." This offer creates in the offeree the *power of acceptance*. Therefore, we say the offeror is the party who makes the offer, and the offeree is the party who has the power of acceptance.

The offer must be stated in language clear enough for a reasonable person to understand that it is an offer. Further, it must be directed to a limited number of offerees.

Once those two criteria are met, the offeree has the power to make a contract (by accepting the offer).

As shown in the flowchart, the offeree has four options following an offer, only one of which immediately results in a contract.

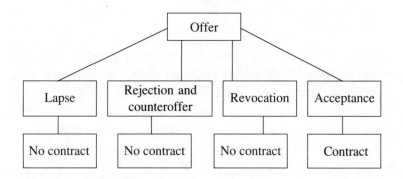

Lapse

I offer to sell you a basset hound puppy. I am the offeror. Suppose you never respond. After a reasonable time, the offer expires. This is called lapse. In effect, too much time kills the offer. Depending on the type of business, lapse may take a long or a short time. For example, an offer to purchase stock expires within minutes, because the market is "wildly fluctuating." An offer to purchase a puppy, however, will stay open for a longer time—for example, two weeks. What is "reasonable" depends on the custom of the business.

Rejection and Counteroffer

Suppose the offeree responds, "I'd really like a puppy, but I can't afford one." This response is a rejection of the offer. Like lapse, a rejection serves to kill the offer. If the offeree responded, "I'd really like a puppy but all I can pay you is $100, not the $200 you are asking," this is a counteroffer. It is also a rejection of the original offer. The new terms now make the offeree the offeror. In effect, the offeree is now saying "I offer to buy your puppy for $100." Notice that this creates in the original offeror the power of acceptance—that is, the power to determine whether contract formation will indeed take place.

Revocation

Suppose I said, "I will sell you a basset hound puppy for $200," but before you could respond, I said, "Never mind!" If the offeror makes an offer and then takes it back that is called revocation of the offer and in effect cancels the offer. Notice that offerors revoke, offerees reject. Revocation must take place prior to acceptance. Once the offeree says "I'll take it," the offeror cannot then revoke. Contract formation has begun.

SECOND ELEMENT: ACCEPTANCE

Suppose the offeror said, "I will sell you a puppy for $200." If the offeree says, "I'd love a puppy! I'll take it!" assent to the terms of the offer has occurred. Contract formation has begun.

Acceptance is one place in contract law where it is significant whether the contract is governed by the UCC or by common law. Under the common law, acceptance must be a mirror image of the offer. If you offer to sell me a house for $450,000, I must use those exact terms in my acceptance. Any deviation from the terms of the offer in the terms of my acceptance constitutes a counteroffer.

Under the UCC, however, if the offeree changes the terms of the offer, there is still a contract. If the parties are not both merchants, the new terms in the acceptance become a proposal that the offeror may accept or reject. If the parties are both merchants, the new terms automatically become part of the contract unless the offeror objects or states that the offer can be accepted only in mirror-image fashion.

Suppose you go downtown to buy a new car. The merchant says, "I

Examples of contract formation

Offeror	Offeree	Result
I am *thinking about* selling my car.	I'll buy it.	No contract. Offer is too vague (language).
I will sell you my car.	No response.	No contract. Lapse.
I will sell you my car.	No.	No contract. Rejection.
I will sell you my car.	Okay.	Contract. Acceptance.
I will sell you my car for $45,000.	How about $35,000?	No contract. Counteroffer.
Okay, I'll take $35,000.	No response.	Acceptance of counteroffer. Valid contract.
Okay, I'll take $35,000.	Now I don't want to buy it.	Contract. Too late to revoke.
Car for sale in newspaper advertisement.	I'll buy it.	Not an offer. No contract. Too many offerees when advertised in newspaper.
Reward in newspaper: $5000 for information leading to the capture of Billy the Kid.	Offeree finds Billy.	Valid contract. Reward contracts are enforceable even if in newspaper. Offerees limited to person who brings in criminal.

will sell you this 1991 Porsche Carrera for $95,000, with a CD player, torsion bar suspension, and a sun roof." You say, "I'll take it, but I also want a leather interior." First, note you are not both merchants. Second, note that you said "I'll take it." This is significant because it constitutes acceptance under the UCC. The fact that you *then* added terms means that you are bound to the contract. The new terms, in this case the leather interior, become a proposal. The offeror may accept or reject that proposal. In any event, however, there is a valid contract.

In the same example, if you were both merchants, the new term would automatically become part of the contract. This is true with three exceptions. If the seller had objected to the leather interior, or stated that the offer could be accepted only with a mirror image, or the new term materially changed the offer, then the new term would not automatically become part of the contract. If none of those exceptions applied, the two parties would have a contract that would include the leather interior.

THIRD ELEMENT: CONSIDERATION

Once a valid offer and acceptance take place, the next element necessary for contract formation is consideration. Basically, consideration means that the promise by the offeror (or promisor) *induced* the offeree (or promisee) to do something that he or she was not *previously, legally bound* to do.

OFFEROR (promisor): I promise to sell you my car.
OFFEREE (promisee): I promise to pay $35,000.

What was the promise by the offeror? To sell the car. What did this promise induce the offeree to do? To promise to pay $35,000. Was the offeree previously bound to pay the money? No. What induced the offeree to promise to pay? The offeror's promise to sell the car.

If you are confused by this, you are certainly not alone. Many legal writers have called for the abolition of consideration as a requirement of a contract. If you study a situation in which there is *not* consideration, however, you may start to see the difference and why it is significant.

OFFEROR: I will buy you a new car.
OFFEREE: Okay, I'll take it.

Did the offeror's promise get the offeree to do anything? Probably not. This is a *gift*. If the offeror does not buy the car, what recourse does the offeree have? Can she hold the offeror to the promise to buy her a car? Probably not. Because there is no consideration, no contract was formed.

Let's change the facts of our example. Suppose the dialogue went like this:

OFFEROR: I will buy you a car.
OFFEREE: I will get an A in my course.

Now, did the promise get the offeree to do something she was not previously, legally bound to do? Probably yes. No one has a legal duty to get an A. The offeror's promise induced the offeree to do something. That is consideration. Now the offeror's promise is enforceable by a court.

Try this example.

CITY OF PORTLAND (offeror): Offers $25,000 reward for information leading to the arrest of criminals A and B.
OFFEREE: Turns in information leading to arrest.

Did the promise by the offeror induce the offeree to do something he was not previously, legally bound to do? If you or I were the offerees, the answer would be yes; there is consideration. But suppose the offeree was a police officer. Can you see why there would be no consideration for the promise to pay? The police officer had a previous, legal duty to supply information. The promise did not induce the officer to do something he wasn't already bound to do. Therefore, he could not enforce this "contract."

Let's briefly summarize consideration. The three elements of consideration (bargained-for-exchange) can be illustrated as follows:

1. Offeror: "I promise to pay you $5000 . . ."
   —This promise must induce the offeree to do something that he or she was not previously, legally bound to do.
2. Offeree: "I promise to paint your house . . ."
   —The promise (by the offeree) to paint the house is the reason why the offeror promised the $5000. That is, the promise by the offeree also got the offeror to do something he or she was not previously, legally bound to do.

Notice that these two parties exchanged promises, probably at the same time. Therefore, each of their respective promises induced a detriment (doing something not previously, legally bound to do) in the other person.

3. There is *either*
   —a benefit to the promisor (in this example, the promisor received a painted house)
   or
   —a detriment to the promisee (in this example, the promisee did something he or she was not previously, legally bound to do).

FOURTH ELEMENT: CAPACITY

The fourth element of all contracts is capacity. This relates to the mental state of the parties to the contract. A party who *lacks capacity* does not have the ability to understand the consequences of entering into a contract.

What would cause someone to lack capacity? As a general rule, a person lacks capacity if he or she is judged by the courts to be mentally ill or if he or she is a minor—under the age of eighteen. For our purposes, we will deal only with lack of capacity due to minority, since it is much more likely that a hotelier will be concerned with that than with mental incapacity.

A minor who enters into a contract may choose to escape his or her contractual liability. This option is called disaffirmance. A person may exercise this right only before reaching the age of eighteen or for a reasonable time thereafter. Suppose that a sixteen-year-old purchases a car on credit, pays for two months, and then decides to return the car. The minor may disaffirm the contract, but must return the car. Then the seller must return to the minor his payments to date. In short, the minor is completely protected. For this reason, few merchants are willing to enter into a contract with a minor.

Once a minor reaches eighteen, the minor reaches "majority" and he or she may want to continue, rather than disaffirm, any contracts entered into before the age of eighteen. In this case, the person now of majority is said to ratify the contract. Ratification can be implied, by retaining the goods, or express, by agreeing orally or in writing to continue the contract. Either way, the person is now liable for performance of a contract entered into as a minor, just as any other adult would be.

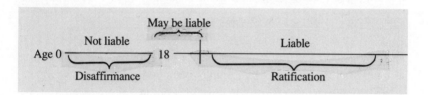

Are minors liable for anything? Yes, in some instances they are liable for their contracts. Most states have specific statutes holding minors liable for particular types of contracts. In general, the courts have ruled that minors are liable for contracts involving necessaries. Necessaries are food, drink, clothing, and *lodging*. Thus, the innkeeper or restaurateur is relatively safe, at least on a contractual basis, for providing these services to a minor. The minor is liable, however, only for the fair market value of such services, which may be considerably less than the price charged by the provider.

FIFTH ELEMENT: LEGALITY

The fifth and final element of a contract is the requirement that the contract be legal. One might expect that what is legal and what is not would be obvious. For example, if a contract's purpose is to provide a room for the night, that is legal. If its purpose is to provide a place for prostitution, that is illegal. If the contract's purpose is illegal, then the contract is unenforceable. There are instances, however, where an *apparently* legal contract may be deemed by a court to be unenforceable.

Examples of Illegal Contracts

Sunday Contracts. In some states, entering into a contract on a Sunday renders the contract void. These laws originated in the religious belief that entering into business transactions on Sunday is immoral. These beliefs were codified in legislation known as Blue Laws and are still in force in some states.

Noncompetition Clauses. Suppose that the Fabulous Hotel hires you as chief chef under a two-year employment contract. After two years, another hotel wants to hire you. In the original employment contract you signed with the Fabulous, the following paragraph appears:

> 22. The below-signed agrees not to work as a chef for another hotel in the same metropolitan area for a period of two years after leaving our employ.

This is called a covenant not to compete, or a noncompetition clause. As a general rule these clauses are legal. Does this mean that you cannot work for another hotel? That depends on certain factors that a court will consider to determine whether the clause is enforceable. These include:

- Whether the agreement stood alone or was contained in an employment contract. If alone, the agreement is void.
- The length of time involved. If too great, the contract is void.
- The location or distance involved. If the contract prohibits you from working in the Western Hemisphere, that is too great. The same county may be a small enough area to enforce the agreement, however.

If you agreed never to be a chef on the entire East Coast for the rest of your life, a court would most likely find that agreement illegal—there is too much time and too great a location involved. A clear dividing line between what is reasonable and what is unreasonable does not exist. The court will study each case individually. You should be aware of the implications of signing such an agreement. The possibility that it will be upheld could prevent you from seeking other employment.

You may see this type of clause not only as an employee but also when you sell a business. Part of the selling contract of your restaurant may be the requirement that you do not open another restaurant in the same city. Again, the courts will look at the same factors mentioned above to determine whether the clause is enforceable.

Exculpatory Agreements. Suppose that you were injured while skiing. On the back of the lift ticket, the resort printed a clause stating "in the event of injury, the resort assumes no responsibility for your injuries." Can you sue for your injuries nevertheless? In many states, an agreement to reduce liability, called an exculpatory clause or waiver, is void. An exculpatory clause, or waiver of liability, states in writing that the owner is not liable for injury to users of the facilities. In New York State, and many other states, these clauses are illegal in specific settings. For example, in New York State, an exculpatory clause at a place of amusement is void. This means that the owner could be sued even if the guest signed the contract saying the owner would not be liable.

Licensing Provisions. Suppose you want to start a business, such as a restaurant. As part of the process of setting up the business, you would need to obtain different licenses, such as a liquor license and a food license. At law, there exist two types of licenses. One type is for the purpose of ensuring competency and the other is a government device for collecting revenues.

Doctors, lawyers, and other professionals must pass a test before the state will award them a license to practice. If these professionals do not obtain a license, but nevertheless enter into a contract, that contract is voidable by the other party. For example: Dr. Jones never passed his medical examinations, but set up his own practice anyway. He sees a patient and sends the patient a bill for his services. That patient may avoid the contract. This means that the patient may choose not to pay because Dr. Jones is unlicensed. Economically, this is a powerful incentive to obtain a license.

The second type of license is one established for the purpose of raising revenue for the state. A bartender's license is an example of the type of license the state uses to collect money, not to establish competency. If a person subject to this type of licensing requirement fails to obtain a license, his or her contracts are still enforceable. Thus, a patron of your restaurant could not argue that your failure to obtain a liquor license excuses her from paying for a pitcher of beer.

Defenses to Contracts

Suppose you have entered into a contract. All five elements are present. Is it possible to escape liability? Sometimes one party to a contract has a legal reason for being excused from contractual liability. This reason is called a defense. While we cannot study all the various defenses, we will examine four of them: fraud, undue influence, duress, and impossibility.

Fraud

Fraud occurs when one party enters into a contract because the other party knowingly lied. Suppose I come to look at your house, which is listed for sale. I ask you if the creek in the back ever floods. You say no. In reliance on your statement, I buy the house. The next spring, the creek floods, causing extensive damage. Can I get out of the contract? Yes. A case of fraud requires proof that:

- One party intended to deceive the other—that is, knowingly lied
- The innocent party relied on the lie
- Reliance was justified

If all those elements are proved, the innocent party can withdraw from the contract. This is called recission. In our example, I (the innocent party) would normally get back my money; you (the guilty party) would get back your house. In other words, the parties are returned to their precontract position.

Undue Influence

Parties to a contract sometimes have a special relationship called a fiduciary relationship. This is a relationship of special trust. As a result, the courts find that the fiduciary is held to a higher standard of care than an ordinary person. For example, a trustee who manages the monies of a young beneficiary is a fiduciary and will be held liable if he or she does anything unethical or illegal with the beneficiary's money. If the trustee uses his or her influence to overcome the will of the other party, that is undue influence. Suppose a trustee talks a beneficiary into investing in one of the trustee's enterprises, which is in fact a high-risk investment, and the beneficiary agrees to the arrangement only because she trusts his judgment. This agreement could be void if the court found that the trustee overcame the "will" of the beneficiary.

DURESS

Duress means forcing a party to enter a contract under threats. Generally, threats of physical or mental harm or threats of criminal prosecution constitute a valid defense to the contract.

Some types of threats are not considered duress, however. For example, threats of a civil lawsuit or ones involving economic need are not valid defenses. A contract entered into under those types of threats would be enforceable.

IMPOSSIBILITY

Suppose a family made reservations at the Fabulous Hotel and then, because of illness, canceled. Or suppose a famous rock group did not show up for a concert you were managing because their bus broke down. Are these excuses recognized by the courts? The answer is, sometimes. Impossibility means, as a general rule, that performance of the contract could be done only at an "excessive or unreasonable cost"—that is, performance is impractical. An earthquake, flood, or emergency that results in a loss of power at the hotel may make the performance of the innkeeper's contract with a guest impractical and, therefore, serve as an excuse for performance.

Contracts That Must Be in Writing to Be Enforceable

Many students are surprised to learn that most oral contracts are enforceable. Of course the problem with enforcing an oral contract is proving its existence. Yet, if this burden can be overcome in court—that is, if the court finds that a contract existed—an oral contract may be enforced.

The phrase "in writing" does not necessarily mean written on a piece of paper. For contracts under the common law, "in writing" means that the contract:

* Identifies the parties
* Describes the subject matter
* Sets forth terms and conditions
* Sets forth the consideration
* Contains the signature of the party to be charged*

For contracts under the Uniform Commercial Code, "in writing" means that the contract:

* Sets out quantity
* Contains enough information for a reasonable person to conclude it is a contract

Many contracts, however, by law *may not* be enforced unless they are in writing. We will now look at three of them, although many more exist.

CONTRACTS FOR THE SALE OF REAL PROPERTY

Real property is land and all things attached to the land (fixtures). Personal property is all other property. If you enter into a contract to sell land, a building, or a house, that contract must be in writing to be enforceable. Are there any exceptions? Yes. Suppose the buyer and

---

*The party to be charged is the defendant in court. Since this is unknown at the time a contract is entered into, it is best to have both parties sign the contract.

seller enter into an oral contract for the sale of a building. The buyer moves in and makes substantial improvements to the property. Although the agreement is oral, the courts will usually find that a contract exists, because people don't usually make improvements unless they own the land. Likewise, a seller would not normally allow such improvement unless he or she owned the land. This situation is called part performance, and it may be sufficient proof of the contract's existence to make the oral contract enforceable.

CONTRACTS FOR THE SALE OF GOODS VALUED AT GREATER THAN $500

Under the Uniform Commercial Code, a contract to sell goods valued at $500 or more must be in writing to be enforceable. Exceptions include part performance. Suppose I agree on the telephone to sell you widgets worth $4000. I deliver $2000 worth, which you accept. You are liable for the payment of $2000 even though the contract should have been in writing.

Another important exception that is used frequently in businesses is the confirming memorandum. Suppose the Fabulous Hotel calls a supplier and orders a thousand luxury terry-cloth robes at a price of $50 each. The contract is for more than $500, and therefore it should be in writing. But the telephone call is, of course, oral. Such an oral contract may be enforceable if one of the parties sends a confirming memorandum and the receiving party does not object within ten days. They have a contract even though it is not "in writing." Remember that in writing under the UCC means that the quantity is stated. If the seller sends a fax, "Order received. Will ship robes as per your order," even though the contract is not in writing by UCC standards (because the order to purchase the robes was oral and the confirmation does not contain quantity) under the confirming memorandum exception, it is an enforceable contract. For this exception to apply, both parties to the contract must be merchants, that is, not private individuals, but businesses who "regularly deal in goods of this kind."

CONTRACTS THAT CANNOT BE PERFORMED WITHIN A YEAR

The third contract that must be in writing is one that cannot be performed within a year. Suppose the Fabulous hires you on March 1, 1991, for one year. You will graduate in May 1991, but you want a little time off to see Europe before you start working. So you agree to begin on August 1, 1991. Does this contract have to be in writing?

Start counting from the day after contract formation. If you agreed to work for the Fabulous on March 1, start to count beginning with March 2. You agreed to work for a year from August 1, 1991, until August 1, 1992. This exceeds one year. March 2, 1991, through August 1, 1992, is almost seventeen months. This contract would have to be in writing to be enforceable.

Damages and Remedies

If the parties to the contract perform all their obligations under the agreement and they have no obligations remaining, they are said to be discharged. Unfortunately, not all parties perform. Failure of a party to perform is a breach. The nonbreaching party may institute a lawsuit and, if so, can choose what to sue for. Damages come in two forms: money damages and nonmoney damages.

MONEY DAMAGES

Compensatory Damages

The nonbreaching party may sue for compensatory damages. These damages will replace the loss to the injured party. For example, suppose a seller fails to deliver tomatoes to the hotel, and purchasing replacement tomatoes costs the hotel an additional $1000. This amount is compensatory damages; $1000 will compensate the buyer for the seller's breach.

Consequential Damages

Suppose the buyer in the above example had also spent $50 on telephone calls, $65 for delivery of the replacement tomatoes, and $35 for additional staff help to deal with the breach. These additional costs are provable as a direct consequence of the breach. Therefore, they may also be recovered, in addition to the compensatory damages.

Nominal Damages

Nominal damages are awarded when the court finds for the non-breaching party in theory but does not find that the nonbreaching party suffered any actual money loss. Usually damages of $1 are awarded in these cases.

Punitive Damages

Some types of money damages generally are not allowable for breach of contract. These include punitive damages, that is, damages whose purpose is punishment. Punitive damages are most often awarded in tort claims, such as negligence actions, not breach-of-contract cases.

Speculative Damages

Speculative damages are usually not allowed either. These are damages remote from the actual agreement. Suppose that the tomatoes mentioned above were a special order and the chef now claims that because they did not arrive on time the number of customers dining that evening was down 10 percent. Damages for such a speculative claim are unlikely to be awarded unless the hotel had conveyed this possibility to the seller at the time the order was placed. It is highly unlikely that such a conversation ever took place. The point is, damages will be too remote unless the buyer and the seller agree otherwise on the liability of the parties at the time of contracting.

NONMONEY DAMAGES

Sometimes money damages are not sufficient compensation for a party's breach. In those instances, the nonbreaching party wants performance of the contract and sues for the remedy called specific performance. Bear in mind that specific performance is not available when money damages would compensate the nonbreaching party; nor is it available to force a party to perform. In other words, you cannot sue to make someone do his or her part under the contract. That would be slavery, which of course is illegal. Let's say that you hire a famous band for the New Year's Eve party at the hotel. If the band cancels, you can sue for money damages—lost customers, loss of provable income. But you cannot sue the band to make them perform at the hotel.

When is specific performance available? When the goods are unique, specific performance is a remedy. Unique goods include land, antiques, and paintings. Thus, you could sue to recover these specific goods, rather than money damages.

THE CONCEPT OF THE DUTY TO MITIGATE DAMAGES

Mitigation (lessening) of damages is a duty imposed by the courts upon the plaintiff, the person bringing the case. Suppose at 3 P.M. the Fabulous Hotel receives a cancellation of a confirmed reservation. Rather than renting the room to the next customer, the hotel lets the room remain empty overnight and then sues the customer who canceled for the full rate. If the hotel had rented the room for the night, it would not have lost any money. The hotel would have lessened (mitigated) its damages. Suppose the hotel could rent the room for only $75, even though the original party had agreed to pay $150. Renting the room at the reduced rate would still be better than letting it sit empty because mitigation would have taken place. In that case, the canceling party would have been liable for $75.

Study Outline for Introduction to Contracts

I.   Overview
II. The laws governing contract formation
    A. Contracts governed by the UCC
    B. Contracts governed by the common law
III. The five elements of a contract
    A. First element: the offer
        1. Offeree options after an offer
            a) Lapse
            b) Rejection and counteroffer
            c) Revocation
            d) Acceptance
    B. Second element: acceptance
        1. Examples of contract formation
    C. Third element: consideration
    D. Fourth element: capacity
    E. Fifth element: legality
        1. Examples of illegal contracts
            a) Sunday contracts
            b) Noncompetition clauses
            c) Exculpatory agreements
            d) Licensing provisions
IV. Defenses to contracts
    A. Fraud
    B. Undue influence
    C. Duress
    D. Impossibility
V.   Contracts that must be in writing to be enforceable
    A. "In writing" defined
    B. Contracts for the sale of real property
    C. Contracts for the sale of goods valued at greater than $500
    D. Contracts that cannot be performed within a year
VI. Damages and remedies

A. Money damages
   1. Compensatory damages
   2. Consequential damages
   3. Nominal damages
   4. Punitive damages
   5. Speculative damages
B. Nonmoney damages
   1. Specific performance
C. The concept of the duty to mitigate damages

Review Questions for Chapter 6

Your answers to the following questions should be based on rules and cases, not on opinion or facts.

1. Mrs. Maxwell greets you by the fountain in the backyard of her lovely mansion, Maxwell House. Upon viewing your baggy slacks and wrinkled shirt, Mrs. Maxwell thinks, "I'll buy you a new wardrobe when you graduate from college." Has an offer been made? State the rule of law that supports your answer.

2. Mrs. Maxwell hands you a cup of tea and says, "I'm so proud of how well you've been doing in your law course. It will be so helpful to you when you graduate. I am considering buying you a new wardrobe." Has an offer been made? State the rule of law that supports your answer.

3. Tired of hearing about your wardrobe, since of course you look smashing, you retire to the gazebo, where you pick up the *Wall Street Journal* and read the following advertisement:

Free to all local college graduates
majoring in hotel management
$1000 coupon toward a new wardrobe.

Has an offer been made? State the rule of law that supports your answer.

4. Mike offers to sell you his Porsche for $2000. State whether a contract has been formed in each of the following situations.

    a. You accept.

    b. You accept. Mike dies.

    c. You say no thanks.

    d. You say, "How about $1500?"

    e. You say, "If you add a stereo."

    f. Before you can reply, Mike says, "Never mind."

5. Assume Arthur and Beatrice are merchants. Beatrice calls Arthur and says, "I'll buy that Porsche you've been wanting to sell for $45,000." Arthur says, "Great. It's yours."

    a. Assume that nothing further happens. Is there a contract?

    b. Assume that after the telephone conversation, Beatrice sends Arthur a note that says, "I'm overjoyed. Thanks." Is there a contract?

6. Janice offers to sell her Porsche to Catherine. The offer states, "I offer to sell you my 1991 Porsche for $89,000 with CD player, leather interior, and torsion bar suspension." State whether a contract exists after each of the responses below. Assume that both parties are nonmerchants.

    a. "I'll buy it, but could you make it $85,000?"

    b. "I'll buy it, but I don't want the leather interior."

    c. Assume that both are merchants. The offeree replies, "I'll take it, and I want a sun roof too."

7. Mr. Ames telephones his son, stating, "If you'll agree to meet me downtown for lunch, I'll buy you that new car you've been wanting so badly." The son meets the father for lunch. Subsequently, the father refuses to buy him the car. Is there consideration?

8. Owens employed Jarrett to drive his car in the Indianapolis 500 auto race. On the day before the race, Jarrett refused to drive Owens's car. Owens then promised to pay Jarrett an additional $5000 if he

would drive. Jarrett agreed. Now Owens refuses to pay. Who will win and why?

9. Driving back to college one snowy evening, a student runs off the road and is injured. A local farmer rushes out to the car, takes the student into his home, and saves his life. The student's father, grateful for all the farmer has done, calls him on the phone after his son recovers and says, "Thank you for all you did for my son. I am so grateful I am going to send you a check for $45,000." Is there a contract?

10. Jeffrey wanted to buy a new car and went to Mercury Motors, where he inspected a 1989 Corvette. Jeffrey had the following conversation with the saleswoman. For each situation, identify whether a defense to the contract exists. You may assume that Jeffrey is twenty-two years old and has mental capacity.

    a. The saleswoman says, "This car is a beauty. She gets 21 miles per gallon." In fact the car gets about 8 miles per gallon.

    b. Jeffrey asks, "Has this car been in any accidents?" The saleswoman replies no. In fact, the car has been totaled and rebuilt twice.

    c. Assume that the saleswoman is also Jeffrey's financial advisor and has been since Jeff was five years old. In addition to handling all of Jeffrey's substantial money, the saleswoman has purchased this car from a friend and is now trying to sell it to Jeff for twice what she paid.

    d. Suppose that the saleswoman says to Jeffrey, "If you don't buy this car I will have some of my friends tie you up and do unspeakable things to you."

11. Ambrose made an offer in writing to purchase the Rundown Hotel and Restaurant. The seller called him back. "Ambrose," he said, "You drive a hard bargain. But I'll sell it to you for the price you're offering." Two days later, Ambrose reads in the paper that the hotel has been sold to another. Does Ambrose have an enforceable contract for the purchase of the hotel-restaurant?

12. Merchant A sent the following note to merchant B: "500."
a. Is this a contract?
b. Suppose the merchant had said instead, "500 cans of tuna. Weds."
c. Suppose the merchant had said, "I promise to send you that tunafish we talked about last week."

13. Steuben was hired by the Fabulous Hotel as the front desk manager. Steuben was hired on May 15, 1991, but was to begin work on August 1, 1991, for a period of one year. Does this contract need to be in writing?

CHAPTER 7

Relationship of Innkeeper and Guest: Creation and Termination

I.   Definition of guest.
     A. "A guest is a transient person who resorts to, or is received at,
        an inn for the purpose of obtaining the accommodations which
        it purports to offer." *Ticehurst v. Beinbrink* (textbook, p. 111).
II. Significance of the innkeeper-guest relationship.
     A. Liabilities do not arise if there is *not* an innkeeper-guest rela-
        tionship (5:8).
III. Other relationships (5:7).
     A. "One who is merely a customer at a bar, restaurant, bar-
        bershop, or newsstand operated by the hotel does not thereby
        establish the relationship of innkeeper and guest" (textbook, p.
        124).
     B. Innkeeper-employee. Employees residing at a hotel are not
        guests (5:21).
     C. Landlord-tenant. Lodgers, boarders, and tenants are not guests
        (5:22).
     D. Licensor-licensee.
     E. Innkeeper-trespasser (5:12). (Note: New York State has abol-
        ished any distinction between guests, licensees, and tres-
        passers. The innkeeper owes them all a duty of care.)
     F. Restaurateur-customer. *Alpaugh v. Wolverton* (textbook, pp.
        122–24).

[77]

IV.   Other nonguests.
    A. Attendee at a ball or banquet and persons hiring banquet rooms for a wedding reception (5:10).
    B. Person at inn for an illegal purpose (5:12). But in *Cramer v. Tarr* (textbook, p. 115), the court ruled that there must be a causal connection between the illegal activity and the damage or loss to the party. If there is no connection, the person may be able to successfully sue the innkeeper as a guest and not as an illegal trespasser.

V.   Factors the courts will consider to determine the existence of the innkeeper-guest relationship (5:1).
    A. Intent of parties to be guests. *Bernard v. Lalonde* (textbook, p. 106).
    B. Acceptance, by inn, of person as a guest. *Langford v. Vandaveer* (textbook, p. 107).
    C. Acceptance by inn of luggage of a person who intends to subsequently register as guest. *Adler v. Savoy Plaza Inc.* (textbook, pp. 111–12).
    D. Registration.
    E. Length of stay. Person staying at hotel for eleven months is not a guest. *Kaplan v. Stogop Realty Co.* (textbook, p. 129).
    F. Method of payment.

VI.   Creation of the innkeeper-guest relationship.
    A. Must have express or implied acceptance by the innkeeper. If the innkeeper refuses to accept the guest, no innkeeper-guest relationship is formed (5:5).
    B. Registration, preregistration, reservations (5:4).
        1. These are contractual in nature. There is an offer by the guest and acceptance by the innkeeper. Consideration paid for the lodgings is the most typical creation of the relationship.
        2. By statute, many states require innkeepers to keep a record of guests—a hotel register (5:15–5:17). In many states, the register must be turned over to law enforcement agents upon request. *Commonwealth v. Blinn* (textbook, pp. 120–22).

C. Implied registration.

   1. An event takes place that would look to a reasonable third party as if the person became a guest of the hotel. (Innkeeper gives guest a room key.)

   2. If one surrenders possessions to an agent of the hotel (a bellhop) and the possessions are accepted, it looks as if (is implied that) the innkeeper-guest relationship has been created.

   3. When the occupant of a room, with the knowledge and consent of the hotel management, turns his room over to another person, and the hotel clerk delivers the room key to that person, he becomes an accepted guest of the hotel. *Moody v. Kenny* (textbook, pp. 117–18).

VII. Duties upon creation of the innkeeper-guest relationship.

A. Liabilities.

   1. Innkeeper becomes insurer of guest's property (textbook, Chapter 12).

   2. Innkeeper has specific standard of care to guest (textbook, Chapter 9).

   3. Certain statutes apply to the relationship (textbook, Chapters 9, 12).

B. The innkeeper has a duty to accept the guest's baggage (5:2) unless:

   1. Items are extremely dangerous.

   2. Items are completely unrelated to the traveler's needs.

   3. Items contain wild or dangerous animals.

C. The innkeeper has no right to investigate the ownership of baggage (5:3).

D. Guests retain their status of being guests even when using the restaurant. *Summer v. Hyatt Corp.* (textbook, pp. 124–26).

VIII. Termination of the innkeeper-guest relationship (5:24).

A. Following payment of the bill and departure of the guest, the innkeeper-guest relationship may continue for a reasonable time within which to remove the baggage or until the baggage is delivered to a common carrier (5:24).

B. In *Salisbury v. St. Regis-Sheraton Hotel Corp.* (textbook, pp. 136–38), even after check-out, innkeeper limitation of liability rules applied for luggage, left in a storage room, that was stolen.

Review Questions for Chapter 7 and Textbook, Chapter 5

Your answers to the following questions should be based on rules and cases, not on opinion or facts.

1. Arthur drives to a distant city and enters the lobby of the Fabulous Hotel. He does not register. He proceeds directly to the Fabulous Hotel's bar, Trader Nick's, but leaves all his luggage in the lobby with an employee of the hotel. After a drink and dinner, Arthur returns to the lobby to enjoy a cigar. He plans to register and looks around for his bags. They are gone.
   a. Is Arthur a guest of the hotel?
   b. Suppose the same facts, except Arthur simply leaves his bags in the lobby but does not turn them over to an employee. Is Arthur a guest of the hotel?
   c. Assume that Arthur is a registered guest. What is the hotel's liability?
   d. Assume that Arthur did not bring his luggage into the hotel, but came into the hotel, had a drink in the bar, ate dinner in the restaurant, and had a cigar in the lobby. He next plans to register. Is he a guest of the hotel prior to registration?
   e. If in scenario d Arthur is not a guest of the hotel, what legal status does he have?
2. Alex is a registered guest of the Friendly Hotel. Two friends from college, Brad and Cecilia, show up to visit him. Alex moves out of the hotel room to stay with some friends in town. Alex tells the night clerk that Brad and Cecilia are taking his room. The night clerk forgets to tell the day clerk. Are Brad and Cecilia guests of the hotel?

3. In the following situations, state whether an innkeeper-guest relationship is created.

   a. Stella, an escapee from the local penitentiary, signs the register under a false name. ?

   b. The Fabulous Hotel has a policy not to admit anyone associated with the Terrible Band, because the last time they stayed there, they destroyed an entire floor. Tommy Terrible, aware of the hotel's policy, registers at the hotel under the name Gary Good.

4. Audrey rents the ballroom of the Ritzy Hotel for her daughter's wedding. During the reception, Audrey slips on water that has collected on the floor from a drip in the ceiling, and she falls. Audrey claims that she is a guest of the hotel and that the hotel owes a higher standard of care to her. Is the hotel liable for Audrey's injuries?

✓the hotel rented the ballroom for a private function, the guests at that function is not a guest at the hotel!

CHAPTER 8

Legal Excuses for Failure to Receive a Guest and Right to Eject

I. General duty to accept all who apply.
    A. The innkeeper has a common-law duty to accept all who apply to the inn for admittance (see Chapter 3 and textbook, Chapters 1–3).
    B. The innkeeper has a statutory duty not to discriminate (see Chapter 5 and textbook, Chapter 4).
II. Reasons the innkeeper can refuse admission to the inn or evict.
    A. There is no room; the inn is filled to normal capacity (6:2).
    B. Persons are of objectionable character (6:3).
        1. The innkeeper should beware of violating discrimination statutes, both state and federal. For example, refusal to admit a couple because they are not married may violate laws prohibiting discrimination on the basis of marital status.
        2. The major concern of the innkeeper is admitting someone who may harm or injure others. The innkeeper can legally refuse admittance to intoxicated, violent, disturbed, or confused individuals and to prostitutes and gamblers (where those activities are illegal).
    C. Guest's inability or refusal to pay (6:4).
        1. It is lawful for the innkeeper to demand payment upon registration, or on a daily basis, or when services are rendered. *Morningstar v. Lafayette Hotel Co.* (textbook, pp. 146–47).

[82]

2. Once admitted, a guest who refuses to pay may be evicted. Usually this is accomplished by locking the person out of his or her room. But there must be an innkeeper-guest relationship. If the charge is excessive and the guest was wrongfully evicted, he or she is entitled to damages for the humiliation.

3. Some states do not allow an eviction for nonpayment. Since eviction is a harsh remedy, the innkeeper should check with legal counsel before evicting a guest.

D. Guest's loss of transient status (6:5).

1. A guest who changes into a tenant may then be evicted under landlord-tenant rules of the state. Usually, these rules call for some type of hearing before eviction.

2. In some states, a guest may be evicted for overstaying. "A person is not entitled to stay indefinitely, and on reasonable notice may be ejected without any other reason" (textbook, p. 147).

3. To prevent these situations the innkeeper should:

   a) Put the length of stay in writing on the registration card.

   b) Clearly state the house rules, defining the duration a guest may remain.

E. Guest's death or illness (6:6).

1. An ill guest may be removed to a place of safety, but removal must be done in a "manner suited to the condition of the ill guest." For a particularly disturbing example of an innkeeper turning a sick guest out of the hotel into cold weather, see *McHugh v. Schlosser* (textbook, pp. 148–50).

2. If a guest dies, the innkeeper must: notify local authorities so that they can investigate; comply with all local ordinances and state laws; and keep an inventory of the deceased's possessions.

F. Persons are unauthorized intruders (6:7).

1. The innkeeper may use reasonable force to eject intruders (e.g., lobby lizards and prostitutes), if he or she believes the intruders may be harmful to guests.

III. Eviction from restaurants.
   A. A restaurant may hire a private security guard to evict patrons staying past a posted time limit. *People on Information of Fanelli v. Doe* (textbook, p. 151).
   B. A restaurant may evict a news team investigating alleged health-code violations; the First Amendment does not protect the media from charges of trespass. *Le Mistral, Inc. v. Columbia Broadcasting* (textbook, pp. 151–53).

Review Questions for Chapter 8 and Textbook, Chapter 6

Your answers to the following questions should be based on rules and cases not on opinion or facts.

1. Four months before spring break, a group of twelve students pooled their money and made plans to stay at the Beach Hotel in Ft. Lauderdale, Florida. No reservations were made in advance, but there were rooms available at the inn. When the students arrived, the innkeeper, seeing that they were students, refused to admit them because in previous years students had caused extensive damage to the premises.
   a. Can the innkeeper lawfully refuse to admit the students? -No
   b. List specific situations in which an innkeeper may lawfully exclude. No room, inn full; people are violent
2. A lieutenant and his wife went from Washington, D.C., to Baltimore and had dinner at the Grand Hotel. During supper, the lieutenant fell ill and suggested to his wife that they spend the night in Baltimore. The husband went to register at the hotel. When the desk staff saw that the couple had no baggage and could not prove that they were married, they refused to admit the couple.
   a. Can the innkeeper lawfully exclude the couple? No
   violate discrimination statutes based on marital status

b. What assumptions do you have to make to answer the first question?

3. Bill and Ann are members of a religious sect that solicits members by going from door to door. They enter the Fabulous Hotel and start soliciting members in a very quiet, unobtrusive manner by knocking on doors and talking to guests. What action can the Fabulous Hotel take?

4. Zimmerman, a registered guest of the Hollywood Hotel, became ill and called the front desk to inform them. The staff at the front desk immediately asked Zimmerman to check out and seek medical attention. The guest explained that he did not feel well enough to leave.

a. What steps should a hotel take in these circumstances?

b. Should a hotel evict a guest in these circumstances?

5. Hopkins registered at the Commerce Hotel for seven days. Nine days later, Hopkins was still in his room and had said nothing to the front desk staff about staying or leaving. Attempts to get in touch with him went unanswered. On the tenth day, the front desk manager went to Hopkins's room, removed his belongings, and changed the "lock" so that Hopkins could no longer gain entrance to the room.

a. What is the proper way to remove an overstay from a hotel room? *give reasonable notice.*

b. Was the action taken against Hopkins legal? Why? *Yes.*

CHAPTER 9

Liability for Failure
to Honor Reservations

I. Innkeeper's common-law duty (7:1).

    A. The innkeeper has a common-law duty to admit all who apply unless they come within one of the defined exceptions. (For a discussion of the exceptions, see Chapter 8 and textbook, Chapter 6.)

II. A reservation as a contract (7:2).

    A. The innkeeper-guest relationship is formed by consent of the parties (consensual) but is not necessarily contractual.

    B. If a guest is a walk-in, the relationship becomes contractual when the innkeeper accepts the guest.

    C. If the relationship is formed by reservation, it becomes contractual *before* the guest arrives because it has the elements of contract formation.

        1. Offer and acceptance = the reservation.

        2. Consideration = guest's confirmation by payment.

III. Contractual duties imposed upon the guest (7:5).

    A. If the guest has a reservation, the guest has the duty to abide by the terms of the reservation agreement.

    B. A guest who cannot show up should cancel, and the hotel should return the deposit unless:

        1. There is an agreement stating otherwise. In *Freeman v. Kiamesha Concord, Inc.* (textbook, pp. 171–72), the guest

[86]

entered into a contract with the Concord Hotel whereby the guest paid for a set amount of time at the hotel. The court found the guest liable for the entire amount paid, even though he checked out earlier and did not receive the value of the services paid for.

2. The innkeeper cannot rerent the rooms. In *2625 Building Corp. v. Deutsch* (textbook, pp. 170–73), the plaintiff reserved and paid for six rooms at the Marriott during the weekend of the Indianapolis 500. Plaintiff canceled the contract and asked for his money back. The court found that plaintiff was entitled to recover his deposit minus any actual damages suffered by the Marriott. Since the Marriott had two months to find others to rent the room, its actual damages should have been minimal.

IV. Damages available if either party breaches the contract (7:2).

A. Compensatory or actual damages.

1. Place the nonbreaching party in as good a position as he or she would have been had there not been a breach. See *McDevitt and Street Co. v. Marriott Corp.* (textbook, pp. 165–68), in which this rule of restitution is discussed.

2. If damages are too "speculative" (too difficult to determine— for example, profits) the court will not award them. However, in *Cardinal Consulting Co. v. Circo Resorts, Inc.* (textbook, pp. 189–93), the court awarded lost profits when a hotel canceled fifty rooms and a travel agent had to cancel prescheduled tours of Las Vegas.

B. Specific performance (7:2).

1. Instead of suing for money damages, the nonbreaching party sues to force the breaching party to perform. This remedy is available only for certain types of goods such as antiques and real property. Not an appropriate remedy when the contract is compensable in money damages.

2. For example, A sues store B for delivery of luggage (specific performance), rather than for money damages. Specific per-

formance is not available for luggage. Money will compensate A. A can buy luggage elsewhere with the money awarded for damages.

C. Liquidated damages.
 1. Set ahead of time by the parties in the contract.
 2. May be allowed if they are closely aligned to the actual damages suffered by the parties.
 3. May include a guest's deposit if the innkeeper cannot rent out the room. *Kona Hawaiian Associates v. The Pacific Group* (textbook, pp. 160–64).

D. Punitive damages (7:7–7:8).
 1. Awarded to the plaintiff in order to punish the defendant. Rarely, if ever, seen in breach-of-contract cases. However, where the action of the innkeeper is "wanton or reckless," these damages are allowed because the behavior is "like a tort." *Reinah Development Corp. v. Kaaterskill Hotel Corp.* (textbook, pp. 181–83).
 2. In *Dalzell v. Dean Hotel Co.* (textbook, p. 178), the hotel mistakenly ejected a paying guest from her room. The court awarded punitive damages (exemplary damages), stating that the action by the hotel amounted to gross and culpable negligence.
 3. In cases involving "bumping" from airlines, the courts have awarded punitive damages, in *Wills v. Trans World Airlines, Inc.* and *Nader v. Allegheny Airlines, Inc.* (textbook, p. 180).
 4. In *Dold v. Outrigger Hotel* (textbook, pp. 185–87) the plaintiffs had reservations at the Outrigger Hotel in Hawaii, but upon arrival were transferred to another hotel of lesser quality. Plaintiffs sought punitive damages, which the court denied; instead the court stated that "where a contract is breached in a wanton or reckless manner as to result in a tortious injury, the aggrieved person is entitled to recover in tort" (textbook, p. 187).

E. Consequential damages (7:6).

1. Flow from the breach, or are a consequence of the breach. Damages in addition to the actual damages suffered. For example, profits may be awarded to the innkeeper when he or she can prove the loss of profits because of last-minute cancellations resulting in an inability to relet the rooms.

Review Questions for Chapter 9 and Textbook, Chapter 7

Your answers to the following questions should be based on rules and cases, not on opinion or facts.

1. Sam and Sylvia called the Fabulous Hotel and made a reservation by telephone for the nights of December 24 and 25. The price of the room per night was $200. When Sam and Sylvia arrived, the hotel apologized because no rooms were available; all had been booked. They made arrangements for Sam and Sylvia to stay at the Cutrate Hotel nearby.
   a. The cost at the Cutrate is $50 per night. Sam and Sylvia paid the cab fare of $15 to go from the Fabulous to the Cutrate and $45 for telephone calls to let friends and business associates know of the new location. Which types of damages are available, if any? What amount is available, if any?
   b. Sam had planned to transact business while staying at the Fabulous Hotel. Now that he is staying at the Cutrate, he is humiliated and embarrassed. As a result, he does not want any of his potential clients to visit him at the hotel. Sam claims that as a result of the breach by the Fabulous Hotel, he has lost potential business contracts worth $500. Which type of damages is Sam seeking? Are they available? How much, if anything, would a jury award for this claim?
   c. Sylvia claims that as a result of the breach by the Fabulous Hotel, she has suffered humiliation and embarrassment in the

amount of $100,000. Which type of damages is Sylvia seeking?
Are they available? How much, if anything, would a jury award
for this claim?

d. Both Sam and Sylvia wish to sue the Fabulous Hotel to punish
them for their behavior. They claim that the actions by the Fabulous Hotel were wanton or reckless. Which type of damages are
they seeking? Are they available? How much, if anything,
would a jury award for this claim?

e. Both Sam and Sylvia wish to sue the hotel for overbooking and
seek your advice on the availability of federal legislation that
might prohibit overbooking. Advise them.

f. Suppose that immediately after Sam and Sylvia made their res-
ervation at the Fabulous Hotel, a hurricane destroyed the hotel.
What excuse does the hotel have for not honoring reservations?
Does the hotel have any liability under this theory?

CHAPTER 10

Innkeeper's Duty to Guest:
Courteous and Considerate Treatment

I. Common-law duties of innkeeper to guest (8:1).
   A. To provide guests with shelter, protection, food, and safe premises.
   B. Courteous and considerate treatment:
      1. A duty to honor the guest's privacy (not to intrude upon guest).
      2. A duty to treat guest in a considerate manner (not to insult guest). The courts have recognized *a right of guests* to be free from insults.
   C. "Courteous and considerate treatment" in this context refers to a *legal* standard and does not necessarily refer to a type of behavior.
II. Innkeeper's right of access to guest's room (8:2).
   A. An innkeeper may enter a guest's room without a warrant and without liability:
      1. Once the rental period is over (8:3).
      2. Once the guest is justifiably ejected (textbook, Chapter 5).
      3. Once the room is abandoned (textbook, Chapter 5).
      4. If the guest fails to pay.
      5. For an emergency (8:2).
      6. To fulfill express and implied duties such as making the beds and providing room service (8:3).

7. To prevent danger to guests (8:2).

B. In *U.S. v. Rambo* (textbook, pp. 203–5), the police entered the defendant's hotel room without a warrant. The court stated that had this been a "properly rented room" Rambo would have enjoyed the protection of the Fourth Amendment. But since Rambo had been ejected from the hotel room for disorderly conduct prior to the search, the rental period had terminated, and control over the hotel room reverted to the management.

III. Guest's right of privacy with regard to room.

A. Fourth Amendment (8:4).

1. In *Sumdum v. State* (textbook, pp. 199–200), the U.S. Supreme Court said the "right of privacy" exists in a hotel room. This means that an employee may not consent to a search of the room during the rental period.

B. Damages for unlawful intrusion (8:7).

1. The innkeeper may be liable in money damages for intrusion into the guest's room. In *McKee v. Sheraton-Russell, Inc.* (textbook, p. 208) the guest was awarded over $5000 for a bellboy's intrusion.

2. The innkeeper may also be liable in damages for the physical discomfort suffered by a guest evicted from an assigned accommodation. *Pollock v. Holsa Corp.* (textbook, pp. 209–10).

IV. Innkeeper's duty regarding privacy of telephones (8:5).

A. Telephone lists are protected by the Fourth Amendment. Police need a warrant to obtain these lists. *People v. Blair* (textbook, pp. 205–6).

B. The hotel may listen to telephone calls if there is a "reasonable belief" that the hotel is being used for an illicit purpose. *People v. Soles* (textbook, pp. 206–7).

V. Authority to identify guest to police (8:6).

A. Innkeepers have no duty to protect their guests from being arrested by the police.

B. But the inn is liable when the arrest is due to false statements of the innkeeper or his or her agents. *Smith v. Jefferson Hotel Co., Inc.* (textbook, p. 107).

VI. Innkeeper's right to assign rooms (8:8).

    A. The innkeeper has the "right to assign the guest to any proper room, and he may at will change the room and assign the guest, with or without his consent, to another room" (textbook, p. 211).

VII. Specific duties *not* owed to guest.

    A. To furnish telephone service (8:10).

    B. To furnish "the key to the inn" and to awaken guest (8:11). *Gumbart v. Waterbury Club Holding Corp.* (textbook, pp. 213–14).

    C. To deliver messages and telegrams (8:12).

        1. An innkeeper who assumes the duty to perform these tasks, however, may be liable for breach of contract if he or she fails to perform.

Review Questions for Chapter 10 and Textbook, Chapter 8

Your answers to following questions should be based on rules and cases, not on opinion or facts.

1. Dunster is the president of a major corporation. She checks into the Urbane Hotel on the night of December 10. At approximately 11 o'clock that evening, an important telegram arrives at the hotel for Dunster, and the hotel staff fails to deliver it to her until December 12. Dunster claims that because she did not get the message immediately she has lost an important business deal, "possibly worth thousands of dollars."

    a. What would be the outcome in a lawsuit by Dunster against Urbane?

    b. Would the hotel's liability be different if Dunster, upon checking in, had informed the night staff that she expected a telegram (or fax) and the staff had promised to deliver it upon arrival?

2. The Millfords checked into the Fiddledeedee Hotel and, after settling into their room, were asked by the manager to move to a different room for no apparent reason. The Millfords refused, claiming that such a request was "outrageous, unkind, and discourteous."

a. Is the hotel liable?

b. Would the Millfords have a valid lawsuit if they had been asked to vacate their room because the room was promised to another?

3. The Big City police suspect that illegal activity is taking place in a hotel room rented to Sam Snide. Without obtaining a warrant, the police:

a. Gain admission to Snide's room with a pass key provided by an employee of the hotel while Snide is absent.

b. Wiretap the telephone in Snide's room and tape conversations.

c. Listen to Snide's telephone conversations on an extension in another room.

d. Search all of Snide's luggage that is stored in the hotel's storage area.

Discuss each of the above actions in terms of its constitutionality, using cases from the chapter. Then consider whether the innkeeper has any liability for the actions of the police.

PART III

TORT LAW: LIABILITY FOR GUEST'S SAFETY

CHAPTER 11

Introduction to Torts:
Duty to Provide Safe Premises

Chapters 9–11 of the textbook cover the liability of an innkeeper for injuries to guests. This chapter begins with a general introduction to the law of torts, followed by an outline of the material that appears in textbook Chapter 9. The next two chapters summarize textbook Chapters 10 and 11.

Torts are civil, as opposed to criminal, wrongs. In a civil action the plaintiff, the person bringing the lawsuit, sues the defendant for *money* damages. In a criminal action, the government brings an action against the defendant, not for money damages, but to incarcerate.

Torts generally can be divided into two categories: intentional wrongs and unintentional wrongs. For purposes of this course, we are going to discuss only the category of unintentional wrongs, or negligence.

Elements of a Negligence Lawsuit

The elements of negligence (9:4) refer to what the plaintiff will have to prove to win the case. There are four elements of a cause of action for negligence:

✓1. Defendant's duty of care
2. Defendant's breach of duty
3. Proximate cause
4. Damages suffered by plaintiff

Suppose that the Luxury Hotel has a beautiful indoor swimming pool. The Sidney family is registered at the hotel, and little Melanie Sidney is happily playing at the poolside when she slips on a beer bottle and falls. She lacerates her leg, and the family incurs $25,000 in medical bills. As you will recall from Chapter 2, the defendant is the hotel, and the plaintiffs are the Sidney family. What will the Sidneys have to prove in order to win their case? Are there any defenses available to the hotel that might lessen or eradicate the damages sought? These are some of the questions we will consider.

1. The defendant has a duty of care (9:1).

A duty of care is the same as a standard of care. This standard is set by laws. Think about when you drive your car. The speed limit, rights of way, and rules regarding pedestrians are all duties of care set by law.

Standards also may be set by an industry. For example, it may be the custom in the hotel business for all revolving doors at the main entrance of large hotels to be monitored by a guard. If a patron is hurt going through the door because a guard was not in place, the hotel did not meet the standard of care set by the industry.

If you have no duty, you cannot be liable for negligence. In our example, it is likely that the Luxury Hotel will be found to have a duty to pick up glass bottles around the pool.

2. The defendant breached the duty of care.

If the defendant has a certain duty (standard of care) and falls below that duty, the defendant is said to have breached the duty of care. If you drive your car 70 miles per hour in a 55-mph zone and injure someone, you have fallen below the duty of care. Likewise, if you drive 40 mph in a 55-mph zone, you may also breach your duty if the weather conditions warranted an even slower speed. The standard is that of a *reasonable person* in a like situation. Would a reasonable person slow down? If so, then the person who did not is in breach.

In our example about the Sidney family what would they have to prove? First, they would have to put other hotel managers on the witness stand and establish that there is a standard in the industry. Those hotel managers would then have to testify that at their hotels, failure to pick up empty bottles by the pool is considered a breach. The standard and the breach are established by the testimony of expert witnesses.

3. The breach caused the plaintiff's injuries (proximate cause).

If there is no causal relationship between the defendant's negligence and the plaintiff's injury, then there can be no liability. Suppose you are driving 70 mph in a 55-mph zone and your passenger has a heart attack. Did your speeding cause the heart attack? To successfully sue you for negligence, your passenger (the plaintiff) would have to prove that it did. In our example, it appears that the Luxury Hotel's failure to clean the pool area caused the plaintiff's injuries. Thus proximate cause exists.

4. The plaintiff suffered injury (damages).

Before a defendant can be liable for negligence, the defendant must cause damages to the plaintiff. Suppose you fire a gun in a heavily wooded, heavily populated area, without first checking to see if any-one is in the vicinity. A reasonable person would most likely check in and around the targets. Thus, you have a duty, and you breached it. If you fire the gun, and no one is injured, however, the fourth element, damages, is missing. Similarly, if Melanie Sidney had slipped on a beer bottle and fallen, but had suffered no injury, the Luxury Hotel would not be liable for negligence. The plaintiff must prove all four elements of negligence to win the lawsuit; if any element is missing, the plaintiff will fail. Let's look at another example.

A guest, John Smith, calls the front desk and tells a staff member that he has just placed his room-service tray outside the door. The staff member fails to tell the housekeeping staff. Another guest, Mar-cia Hunt, trips on the tray in the hall, some two hours after John's phone call, and is injured by shards of glass. Is the hotel liable? Most likely you immediately answered yes. Now that you are familiar with the four elements of negligence, analyze the problem with them in mind.

First Marcia must prove that the hotel had a duty of care. How would she prove that? Probably by putting other hotels' personnel on the witness stand to testify about their standard operating procedure with regard to room-service trays. Suppose these other hotels testify that they have a three-minute pick-up time? If that is true, our hotel appears to have breached the standard, or custom, in the business; our hotel fell below the standard. Did that breach cause the injury? Did leaving the tray outside the door cause Marcia to stumble and fall? If the answer is yes, and assuming that Marcia had a physical injury, then all four elements have been proved in favor of the plaintiff.

Defenses to a Negligence Lawsuit

So far, we have analyzed the negligence lawsuit from the plaintiff's point of view. As a manager, you need to be aware that there are defenses available to a negligence lawsuit. Some of the defenses to a negligence lawsuit are discussed below.

ASSUMPTION OF THE RISK

If the plaintiff had actual knowledge of a risk and voluntarily exposed himself or herself to it anyway, the plaintiff is said to have assumed the risk of injury. Suppose the plaintiff is injured sky diving, or boxing, or skiing. The courts generally consider those activities risky and hold that the plaintiff assumes at least a part of the risk of being injured by participating in those activities. As a result, usually a court will not allow the plaintiff to recover.

COMPARATIVE NEGLIGENCE

Most states have adopted the rule of comparative negligence. It states that if a *plaintiff* is in any way negligent, the plaintiff's amount of negligence will be deducted from the money award. Suppose that in the room-service example above Marcia was ten years old and was running up and down the hall before the accident. If the jury finds that the plaintiff was entitled to $100,000 for her injuries but was also 10 percent negligent the amount of the plaintiff's negligence will be subtracted from the plaintiff's judgment as follows:

Award to plaintiff ($) − Plaintiff's negligence (%) = Final award to plaintiff
$100,000 − (10% × $100,000) = $90,000

CONTRIBUTORY NEGLIGENCE

A few states follow the doctrine of contributory negligence, which states that if the plaintiff was at all negligent, he or she can recover nothing. In our service-tray example, Marcia was assessed by the jury as being 10 percent negligent. If this accident occurred in a state that follows the doctrine of contributory negligence, Marcia could recover nothing.

LACK OF ONE OR MORE OF THE FOUR ELEMENTS

If any one of the four elements of negligence is missing, then the plaintiff cannot recover.

ILLEGAL PURPOSE

Even if a guest has an illegal purpose for being on the premises, the innkeeper may be liable to that guest provided that the injury is unrelated to the illegal activity. For example, a guest registers under a false name and then dies in a fire on the premises caused by the inn's negligence. Since the false registration and the death are unrelated, the estate of the deceased may still recover for the inn's negligence. If the guest is on the premises to steal from rooms, however, and is injured while engaged in this illegal behavior, no recovery is allowed because the illegal activity is related to the injury.

Negligence *Per Se*

If the defendant violates a statute and the four elements of negligence are present, the defendant is negligent *per se*. Negligence *per se* means that a statute exists mandating a certain behavior and that by violating the statute, the defendant has fallen below the standard. For example, suppose that a local building code mandates grade A wiring in hotel alarm systems, but the hotel installs grade B. In a lawsuit brought by guests injured in a fire, the duty and the breach are already proved because of the breached statute.

Doctrine of *Res Ipsa Loquitur*

In negligence cases, the *plaintiff* has the burden of proving the four elements. In a case alleging *res ipsa loquitur* ("the thing speaks for itself"), however, the plaintiff is alleging that the injury would not have happened but for the negligence of the defendant even though the plaintiff cannot prove specific acts of negligence. This allegation puts the burden of proof on the *defendant*. For example, we say that the crash of an elevator is *res ipsa loquitur* because elevators do not crash unless someone was negligent. In *Deming Hotel Co. v. Prox* (textbook, p. 227), a mirror fell off a wall. The facts required the defendant hotel to explain that it was not negligent; in other words, the defendant had the burden of proving its innocence, as opposed to a routine negligence case in which the burden of proof is on the plaintiff (to prove the defendant's negligence).

Outline of Textbook Chapter 9—Duty to Provide Safe Premises

I. Duty of the innkeeper (9:1).
    A. The innkeeper has a duty of reasonable care toward his or her guests.
    B. The innkeeper is not an insurer of liability. This means that the innkeeper is not held to a standard of care whereby the innkeeper *guarantees* one's safety in the inn. The innkeeper is not liable unless he or she is negligent.
II. Examples of negligence lawsuits.
    A. Floors and railings (9:11)
        1. The innkeeper is liable only if the plaintiff can show a defect such as negligent construction *plus* notice to the hotel.

2. In *Williams v. Carl Karcher Enterprises, Inc.* (textbook, pp. 233–36), a wet floor was held to be a defect. The restaurant "floor should have been dried by hand, roped off, or cleaned before or after business hours."

B. Exterior passageways, walks, and stairways (9:13).

　　1. The innkeeper is liable if he or she knows of the following conditions and does nothing to warn or correct:

　　　　a) Dangerous staircase. *Allgauer v. Le Bastille, Inc.* (textbook, p. 240).

　　　　b) No handrail on stairs. *Luxen v. Holiday Inns, Inc.* (textbook, pp. 240–41).

　　2. The innkeeper is not liable if the condition is obvious. *Buck v. Del City Apartments* (textbook, p. 240).

　　3. The innkeeper is not liable if a defect (in stairs) cannot be proved. *Campbell v. Bozeman Community Hotel* (textbook, p. 240).

C. Doors (9:12).

　　1. The innkeeper is liable for unmarked glass doors.

　　2. There should be a doorperson to supervise busy, revolving doors. *Schubart v. Hotel Astor, Inc.*, 168 Misc. 431, 5 N.Y.S.2d 203 (Sup. Ct. 1938), *aff'd mem.*, 255 App. Div. 1012, 8 N.Y.S.2d 567 (2d Dep't 1938), *aff'd mem.*, 281 N.Y. 597, 22 N.E.2d 167 (1939).

　　3. Sticking door not negligence. *Winkler v. Seven Springs Farm, Inc.* (textbook, pp. 237–39).

　　4. Sliding glass doors that knocked down elderly woman, negligence. *Landmark Hotel and Casino, Inc. v. Moore* (textbook, p. 239).

　　5. Liability for child's slip and fall through sliding glass doors constructed from plate glass. *Jenkins v. McLean Hotels, Inc.* (textbook, p. 239).

D. Furnishings and equipment (9:9, 9:10).

　　1. The innkeeper must maintain appliances, furniture, and plumbing fixtures.

2. The innkeeper may not delegate that duty to another (9:7). *Page v. Sloan* (textbook, pp. 224–26).

3. In *Dillman v. Nobles* (textbook, pp. 228–29), the hotel was found liable for injuries sustained when a broken chair caused a fall.

4. Innkeepers have a duty to inspect; there is no liability if there is no problem apparent upon a reasonable inspection.

5. In *Davis v. Alamo Plaza of Shreveport, Inc.*, 253 So. 2d 232 (La. App. 1971), the hotel was not held liable for a guest's fall caused by a defect in the carpet of which the innkeeper was unaware.

E. Plumbing or bathroom fixtures (9:14).

1. The innkeeper is liable:

   a) For burns if the water is too hot.

   b) If handles break off from the wall in the tub. *Apper v. Eastgate Association* (textbook, pp. 242–44).

   c) If no efforts are made to prevent falls.

F. Fire precautions (9:15).

1. In *Northern Lights Motel, Inc. v. Sweaney* (textbook, pp. 245–48), failure to meet fire and building code standards was held to be negligence *per se*.

2. In *Altamuro v. Milner Hotel, Inc.* (textbook, pp. 249–55), the hotel was held liable for a death caused by a fire arising from the negligence of an employee.

3. In *Taieb v. Hilton Hotels Corp.* (textbook, pp. 255–58), the hotel was held liable for injuries resulting from its failure to have employees assist guests in the stairwell during a fire.

G. Vermin, insects, animals (9:15).

1. In *DeLuce v. Fort Wayne Hotel* (textbook, p. 261), the court stated that a hotelkeeper could be held liable for a rat bite on the ground of negligence *per se* if the hotelier "knew or should have known" of the presence of rats.

2. In *Del Rosso v. F. W. Woolworth Co.* (textbook, pp. 261–62), the restaurant was not held liable for a rat attack at a

Woolworth's lunch counter because the defendant did not know of the presence of rats.

3. In *Brasseaux v. Stand-By Corp.* (textbook, pp. 262–63), the defendant was held liable for a slip-and-fall injury caused by a bee attack because the defendant hotel knew of the presence of the bees, but did not warn the guest or eradicate the bees.

H. Areas outside the inn (9:18).

1. In *Withrow v. M. C. Woozencraft*, 90 N.M. 48, 559 P.2d 425 (1976), the innkeeper was held liable for a fall resulting from inadequate lighting combined with a dangerous sidewalk outside the motel room.

2. In *Marhefka v. Monte Carlo Management Corp.* (textbook, pp. 263–64), the innkeeper was held liable for an injury on wooden steps leading from the beach to the ocean.

3. In *Barber v. Princess Hotel International Inc.* (textbook, pp. 265–66), the innkeeper was not held liable for a riding accident that took place off the premises and not under the supervision of the hotel.

4. In *Beauregard v. Barrett* (textbook, p. 266), the innkeeper was not held liable for the hip injury of a guest who wandered off the premises and fell.

5. In *Eldridge v. Downtowner Hotel* (textbook, pp. 267–68), the innkeeper was not held liable for the injuries of a guest "mooning" and falling off a balcony.

I. Parking lots (9:19).

1. In *Larrea v. Ozark Water Ski Thrill Show, Inc.* (textbook, pp. 269–70), the defendant was not held liable for plaintiff's slip and fall in a parking lot in "open and obvious condition."

2. In *Rappaport v. Days Inn of America, Inc.* (textbook, pp. 270–72), the innkeeper was held liable for an inadequately lit parking lot.

III. Duty of the innkeeper to child guest (9:16).

A. The innkeeper has a higher standard of care toward children.

B. In *Baker v. Dallas Hotel Co.* (textbook, pp. 258–60), the hotel was not held liable for a child's fatal fall from a window, because "screens on the window are meant to keep insects out, not children in."

Review Questions for Chapter 11 and Textbook, Chapter 9

Your answers to the following questions should be based on rules and cases, not on opinion or facts.

1. Emory, a guest at the Fabulous Hotel, was leaving the hotel through a back exit when a thief approached him, knocked him down, and stole his watch, wallet, and cuff links. Emory claims that the hotel was negligent in not posting a guard at the exit. Outline what Emory would have to prove in order to prevail in a lawsuit against the Fabulous Hotel.

2. After a few drinks at the bar of the Dry Gulch Motel, Jill decided to go swimming in the motel's pool. It was 3 o'clock in the morning. The pool was in a fenced-in area, and a sign clearly stated the hours that the pool was open: from 9 A.M. to 9 P.M. Jill, disregarding the sign, climbed over the fence and swam in the pool. Upon exiting, she stepped on a broken beer bottle that someone had left poolside, severely lacerating her foot. Discuss both sides of a lawsuit, assuming that Jill is the plaintiff and the Dry Gulch is the defendant. Be sure to discuss all the defenses available to the motel.

3. Upon completion of the new multimillion-dollar Casino Hotel, the general manager noticed a burning smell in some of the lounge areas. She called a local electrician, who inspected the premises and rewired the rooms. Shortly thereafter fires broke out in those rooms and several people were injured. The Casino Hotel claims that since it took every precaution and hired an electrician, the lawsuits should be against the electrician, not against the hotel. Discuss the validity of this claim.

4. The Playland Hotel has decided to market itself as a family hotel, complete with pools of various sizes and game rooms appealing especially to youngsters and teenagers. As legal counsel to the Playland, how would you advise its management with regard to their liability regarding these forms of entertainment? Regarding their attractiveness to children?

5. After a rainy day in the city, the PishPosh Hotel's main entrance was wet and slippery. A janitor was assigned the duty of constantly mopping, but with the flow of traffic through the doors, it became impossible to keep up. Discuss the liability of the hotel in the following situations.

    a. A guest of the hotel slips and falls in the water.

    b. The hotel posts signs in the water saying CAUTION. Shortly thereafter, a guest slips and falls.

    c. A nonguest (trespasser or licensee), on his way to another building, slips and falls in the puddle.

    d. An intoxicated trespasser, heading for the lobby to sit down and dry off, slips and falls in the puddle.

6. Assume that in each of the following situations you are the legal counsel for the hotel. Also assume that the only cause of action the hotel is threatened with is negligence. Analyze each of the claims below by discussing the individual elements of negligence. Are all four elements present in each of the following scenarios?

    a. A guest threatens to sue because her check-in at the hotel took over fifteen minutes.

    b. A guest of the hotel wants to sue for an injury sustained when she tripped going up the stairs to the lobby. The management inspects the carpet, and it is properly tacked down.

    c. A driver on the street outside the hotel loses control of his car and crashes into the lobby of the hotel. Several guests sitting in the lobby are injured, and the ambulance and paramedics arrive. Another guest of the hotel, witnessing these events, suffers a heart attack. If all these guests of the hotel wish to bring lawsuits against the hotel, which are likely to be successful?

CHAPTER 12

Liability of Resort Facilities

I. General rule (10:1).
   A. A resort is different from a hotel because it has additional services.
   B. Nevertheless, similar responsibilities are laid down; that is, the innkeeper of a resort facility is not an insurer of safety, but must use ordinary care toward guests.
   C. However, if you make the premises more attractive for people to use, you are also likely to make more money, and some courts hold that as a result, resorts should have more liability.

II. The standard of care of a resort (10:1).
   A. The owner must use ordinary care toward guests in the construction, maintenance, and operation of the facility.
   B. The owner will be liable:
      1. On actual notice of a defect.
      2. If he or she has constructive notice of a defect (should have known upon a reasonable inspection).

III. Duty.
   A. Warn of concealed perils that are foreseeable (10:2–10:3).
      1. Powerful, surging surf. *Tarshis v. Lahaina Investment Corp.* (textbook, pp. 278–79) and *Fuhrer v. Gearhart by the Sea, Inc.* (textbook, pp. 282–86).
      2. Shallow water or low tide. *Blankenship v. Davis* (textbook, pp. 279–80).

       3. Concrete on the bottom of the ocean floor. *Montes v. Belcher* (textbook, pp. 286–88).

B. Supervise the facilities and prevent dangerous conduct (10:5, 10:7).

       1. In *McKeever v. Phoenix Jewish Community Center* (textbook, pp. 290–91), the pool was not held liable for a child's drowning because the lifeguard got to the scene of the accident as fast as humanly possible and made every effort possible to revive the child.

       2. In *Cohen v. Suburban Sidney-Hill, Inc.* (textbook, p. 291), the pool was not held liable for a fall from a slippery ladder.

       3. In *Ginsberg v. Levbourne Realty Company, Inc.* (textbook, pp. 292–93), no liability was assigned for a fall on a basketball court that had a miniscule amount of sand.

       4. In *Allon v. Park Central Hotel Co.* (textbook, pp. 293–94), a hotel was found to have improperly supervised the pool and thus was held liable for the plaintiff's injuries sustained when a user of the pool did a back dive and collided with the plaintiff.

       5. In *Gordon v. Hotel Seville, Inc.* (textbook, p. 300), a hotel was held liable for injuries sustained by the plaintiff when one guest threw another guest on top of the plaintiff in the hotel pool.

       6. In *Bauer v. Saginaw County Agricultural Society* (textbook, pp. 294–95), the court ruled that a fairgrounds owner failed to supervise the premises and thus was liable for injuries to a patron who was shot by a gun discharged in the fair's shooting gallery.

C. Comply with statutory duties (10:8).

       1. Swimming pool statutes requiring posted depth and telephone numbers. *Haft v. Lone Palm Hotel* (textbook, pp. 302–10).

       2. Violation of laws regarding pool water treatment leading to cloudy water and death of guest. *First Overseas Investment Corp. v. Cotton* (textbook, pp. 310–12).

D. Maintain safe premises.
  1. Swimming pools (10:1, 10:9).
     a) In *Hooks v. Washington Sheraton Corp.* (textbook, pp. 274–77), the pool operator was held liable for injuries suffered by an eighteen-year-old boy who dived from an unsafe diving board.
     b) Failure to provide a lifeguard, to erect a hole-free fence, to place a cover on the pool, and to provide lifesaving equipment was held to be negligence in *Gault v. Tablada* (textbook, pp. 313–17).
E. Select competent employees (10:10).
  1. The employer is held to a duty of reasonable care to hire and select competent employees.
  2. In *Ellingsgard v. Silver* (textbook, pp. 320–21), the innkeeper was not held liable for an employee who suffered a heart attack while operating a motor boat, which subsequently struck and injured the plaintiff, because the heart attack was not foreseeable.
IV. Death or injury as presumption of negligence (10:6).
  A. Failure to provide a lifeguard was held to be a question of negligence for the jury to consider in the drowning death of a nineteen-year-old boy in *Rovegno v. San Jose Knights of Columbus Hall Association* (textbook, p. 295–96).
  B. The hotel was held liable for a drowning caused by inappropriate pool maintenance in *Brown v. Southern Ventures Corp.* (textbook, pp. 297–99).
V. Defenses.
  A. Contributory negligence of patron (10:11).
    1. A guest cannot recover if he or she knew or should have known of the danger.
    2. It was held in *Ryan v. Unity, Inc.* (textbook, p. 322) that a guest's being drunk in the pool at night, when visibility is low, is contributory negligence.
    3. Jumping off a high wall into the ocean was considered con-

tributory negligence in *Biltmore Terrace Associates v. Kegan* (textbook, pp. 322–23).

4. An intoxicated health club member who dove off a lifeguard tower into the pool and died was held in a dissenting opinion in *Mullery v. Ro-Mill Construction Corp.* (textbook, pp. 323–26) not to be contributorily negligent, because the club had a duty to remove him from the pool.

B. Assumption of the risk (10:12).

1. In *Sunday v. Stratton Corp.* (textbook, pp. 328–29), a ski resort was held liable for injury to a novice skier who caught his ski on a piece of snow-covered brush. The skier did not assume the risk of imperfectly groomed trails.

2. The doctrine of assumption of the risk has been abolished in Louisiana. The doctrine of comparative negligence allows the jury to reduce the plaintiff's damages by the amount of the plaintiff's own negligence. Assumption of the risk can no longer be used as a bar to the plaintiff's recovery. *Murray v. Ramada Inns, Inc.* (textbook, pp. 332–44).

Review Questions for Chapter 12 and Textbook, Chapter 10

Your answers to the following questions should be based on rules and cases, not on opinion or facts.

1. The Fabulous Hotel turned up the hot water heater in its facilities as winter weather approached so that the highest temperature of the hot water was reached when the coldest weather of the year arrived. Unknown to the hotel, the thermometer on the boiler that supplied the hot water malfunctioned. As a result, the hotel's hot water reached a scalding temperature and burned a guest. Discuss the hotel's liability for the injuries.

2. What is the distinction between contributory negligence, compar-

ative negligence, and assumption of the risk? How is assumption of the risk effected as a defense in a state that has adopted a comparative negligence statute?

3. What is the difference between the liability of the owner of a hotel and that of the owner of a resort? As the owner of a resort, what preventive measures could you take to decrease your liability?

CHAPTER 13

Responsibility for Conduct
of Persons in the Inn

I. Overview.
    A. This chapter does not cover issues arising from a defect in the premises, but instead covers injuries arising when:
        1. A guest is injured by a third party (e.g., an intruder or a burglar).
        2. A guest is injured by an employee of the hotel.
        3. A nonguest is injured.
II. Determining the innkeeper's duty (11:1).
    A. The innkeeper's standard of care will vary according to the particular circumstances and location of the hotel.
    B. Factors the court will consider when determining the innkeeper's negligence.
        1. Size and layout of the complex. *Anderson v. Malloy* (textbook, p. 351).
        2. Accessory uses; ease of entrance; dark and secluded stairwell. All were evidence of a hotel's negligence leading to an attack on a female plaintiff in *Orlando Executive Park, Inc. v. P.D.R.* (textbook, pp. 351–54).
        3. Check-in window located in parking lot of hotel. Held to unreasonably increase risks of attack in *Davenport v. Nixon* (textbook, pp. 354–55).
        4. Prior incidences of criminal activity. *Urbanov v. Days Inns of*

[114]

America, Inc. (textbook, p. 355) and *Garzilli v. Howard
Johnson's Motor Lodges, Inc.* (textbook, p. 355).

5. Allowing persons on the "fringe of the law" to enter hotel.
Put hotel on notice of potential criminal activities in *Virginia
D. v. Madesco Investment Corp.* (textbook, p. 355).

6. Allowing suspicious persons to roam unsupervised. *Peters v.
Holiday Inns, Inc.* (textbook, p. 357).

C. Standards of care the courts will apply to determine the innkeeper's duty to protect the guest.

1. Whether there is some probability of harm sufficiently serious
that a reasonable person (i.e., the innkeeper) would take precautions to avoid it. In *Knodle v. Waikiki Gateway Hotel, Inc.*
(textbook, pp. 357–61) a flight attendant was murdered in the
hotel on the way up to her room.

2. Prior knowledge of danger. But in *Knott v. Liberty Jewelry
and Loan Inc.* (textbook, pp. 361–62), knowledge that a
guest carried a gun was not by itself considered sufficient
evidence that the attacker had a dangerous character and that
the innkeeper had a duty to warn.

3. Foreseeability.

   a) In *Zerangue v. Delta Towers*, 820 F.2d 130 (5th Cir.
   1987), the court held that a security guard could have fore-
   seen the danger to the plaintiff, who exited the hotel, was
   locked out, and subsequently was raped on the street.

   b) Evidence of multiple robberies in the area, personal
   knowledge by hotel staff of "motel bandits," and location
   of motel near a major highway were all considered factors
   that made robbery foreseeable in *Crinkley v. Holiday Inns,
   Inc.* (textbook, p. 367).

D. To whom does the innkeeper owe a duty of protection?

1. The innkeeper owes no duty to protect a trespasser being arrested by federal agents. *Alster v. Palace Co.* (textbook, p.
366).

2. In *Wright v. Webb* (textbook, p. 366), the innkeeper was not

held liable for an attack on an invitee at an adjacent dinner theater. The court held that a business does not have a duty to protect an invitee against criminal assault unless it knows assaults are occurring or are about to occur.

3. In *Holly v. Meyers Hotel & Tavern, Inc.* (textbook, p. 405), the New Jersey Supreme Court held that an innkeeper was not liable to strangers for objects thrown out of hotel windows by guests (11:15).

4. But in *Connolly v. Nicolet Hotel* (textbook, pp. 405–8), the innkeeper was held liable for an object thrown from the hotel, causing a stranger to be blinded in one eye, because prior incidents indicated the rowdiness of guests (water thrown out of hotels, mule in lobby, guns fired in lobby, alligator in hall, bottles thrown in and about hotel).

E. Landlord's duty of care (11:3).

1. Although the landlord-tenant relationship is not the same as the innkeeper-guest relationship, landlord-tenant cases are affected by and can in turn affect innkeeper-guest cases.

2. In *Totten v. More Oakland Residential Housing, Inc.*, 63 Cal. App. 3d 528, 134 Cal. Rptr. 29 (1976), it was held that a landlord may not be held liable for injuries inflicted on a stranger who happens to be on the premises by the criminal attack of other strangers.

3. In *Lay v. Dworman* (textbook, pp. 370–73), it was held that a landlord may be liable for injuries caused to a tenant, by the criminal actions of a stranger, when the landlord is aware of previous criminal activities and a faulty lock on tenant's door.

III. Protection of guests from employees (11:4).

A. The law holds the employer responsible for torts (not crimes) committed by an employee. This is called the doctrine of *respondeat superior* (11:9).

B. *Respondeat superior* (the master answers in money damages for the torts of his servants) pertains to the innkeeper's liability when an employee injures a guest of the hotel (or others). Note how this differs from the section above in which an innkeeper had liability for the actions of a third (unrelated) party such as an intruder or a burglar.

C. For the employer (master) to be liable for the torts of the employee (servant) under the doctrine of *respondeat superior* two elements must be met.
   1. There must be an employer-employee relationship.
   2. The employee must be "acting within the scope of employment," "furthering the master's business."

D. In a few states the employer is liable for the actions of an employee on the basis of a contract theory (implied that the guest be treated with due care and consideration).

E. If the tort is intentional, as a general rule, the master is not liable. Most commonly, liability is for negligence.

F. Examples of employer's liability for an employee's torts.
   1. In *Sheridan v. Hotels Statler Co., Inc.* (textbook, pp. 377–78), a doorman's accidentally closing a guest's hand in a car door was held to be negligence.
   2. *Riviello v. Waldron* (textbook, pp. 381–84), involved an employee's flipping a pocketknife, which accidentally struck a tavern guest in the eye, causing him to lose the use of the eye. In deciding the case, the court considered the likelihood (foreseeability) that that employee might have caused *some* injury in the course of his duties.
   3. In *Cappo v. Vinson Guard Services, Inc.* (textbook, p. 385), the court held the defendant restaurant liable for its parking-lot guard's striking a guest.
   4. In *Boles v. La Quinta Motor Inns, Inc.* (textbook, p. 391), a motel was held liable for its desk clerk's sarcastic and inattentive response to a guest who called in to report she had been raped.
   5. Once a hotel comes to the aid of a guest, the innkeeper will be liable if the assistance puts the guest in a worse position. *Stahlin v. Hilton Hotels Corp.* (textbook, pp. 390–91).

6. In *Soldano v. O'Daniels* (textbook, p. 394), a tavern was held liable for its bartender's refusal to call the police to assist a murder victim in a bar across the street.

7. A hotel may be liable, due to actions of employees, for the suicide of a guest (11:13). *Sneider v. Hyatt Corp.* (textbook, pp. 396–97).

IV. Restaurant keeper's duty to protect patrons (11:14).

A. Restaurants have a duty of ordinary care. If there have been prior incidents, then the duty of care increases, and the restaurant must take steps to protect its customers.

B. Examples.

1. In *Eastep v. Jack-in-the-Box* (textbook, pp. 397–401), the court held the defendant restaurant liable for injuries received in a fight between customers, because the manager failed to evict the patrons despite swearing and physical signs of intoxication and employees stood around watching rather than immediately calling the police.

2. In *Heathcote v. Bisig*, 474 S.E.2d 102 (Ky. 1971), a bartender's failure to eject assailants who beat up a bar patron and to call the police was held to be negligence.

3. In *Alonge v. Rodriquez* (textbook, p. 401), a bar was held liable for injuries sustained by a patron in a brawl among drunken patrons.

4. In *Allen v. Babrab, Inc.* (textbook, pp. 401–2), a tavern owner was held liable for a fight in the parking lot because the club had a history of violence and the owner knew or should have known of the likelihood of violence.

5. In *Gould v. Taco Bell* (textbook, pp. 403–4), the court held that a restaurant manager's failure to prevent a fight or to call the police, despite regular incidents of fights in the restaurant, may lead to liability for punitive damages.

V. Movement toward absolute liability (11:16).

A. Courts are increasingly finding liability for injuries to or death of guests due to both negligent hiring and the failure to maintain safe premises. *Banks v. Hyatt Corporation* (textbook, pp. 410–11).

B. Suggestions when hiring.
   1. Run extremely tight security checks of all prospective employees.
   2. Document all security checks.
   3. Hire security guards through a bonded agency.
   4. Select competent employees.
C. Suggestions for security.
   1. Maintain competent staff.
   2. Maintain adequate security personnel.
   3. Summon police immediately; respond quickly to guests' reports of injuries to other guests.
   4. Design and maintain safe premises, including good locks on the guests' doors, closed-circuit TV, entrance through the lobby.
   5. Warn of dangers and dangerous people.
   6. Maintain safety in the rooms as well as in the lobby.
   7. Illuminate all areas adequately.

Review Questions for Chapter 13 and Textbook, Chapter 11

Your answers to following questions should be based on rules and cases, not on opinion or facts.

1. The Fleabag Hotel is located in a high-crime area of a major city. The Plush Hotel is located in a low-crime area of the same city. You have been hired by both hotels to review security plans for the upcoming years.
   a. What events could have occurred at each of these hotels in the past few years that would influence your security recommendations? List the events and the corresponding recommendations you would make.

b. Do these hotels have different standards of care to their respective guests? If so, what are they?

2. The Sandy Hotel in Tropical, Florida, is designed with the tropical climate in mind. For example, screens rather than glass are used on windows and doors. In the fifty-year history of the Sandy, not one crime has been committed on the premises. Unfortunately on the night of December 16, at the beginning of the Christmas season, plaintiff was assaulted in her room by an unknown assailant. Discuss the liability of the hotel and any defenses available to the hotel.

3. Wally, the wild bellhop, is employed by the Plush Hotel. Driving a van owned by the Plush, and transporting five guests of the hotel, Wally drove the van into a retaining wall, causing injury to the guests. Upon a subsequent blood test, the hotel discovered that Wally was legally drunk at the time of the accident. The five guests want to sue the Plush Hotel.

a. What theories are available to the guests?
b. What do the guests have to prove to prevail?
c. Is Wally liable for anything?
d. What defenses are available to the hotel?

PART IV

RESPONSIBILITY FOR PROPERTY OF GUESTS AND PATRONS

CHAPTER 14

Introduction to the Law of Property

Why Study Property Law?

You may wonder about the applicability of property law to your studies of hotel management. This overview gives you some examples of problems pertaining to property issues that can arise in the hotel and restaurant contexts.

First, if you are interested in buying and selling properties, the knowledge of real property concepts is essential. *Real* property is defined as land and all things attached thereto. "Things attached thereto" are otherwise known as fixtures. The abbreviated definition of real property is land and fixtures. The purchase of a hotel is the purchase of real property—the hotel is firmly affixed to the land and is therefore a fixture. If you are interested in pursuing a career in property development and management, the study of real property has special relevance to your career.

A hotelier or restaurateur, on the other hand, comes into contact daily with *personal* property. Personal property is defined as all property that is not land and fixtures. Your premises will contain personal property, your guests will lose, damage, and destroy personal property, and you will seek insurance for personal property. It is around you all the time. You will hear claims that your employees have injured or lost a patron's property, and you will probably post signs disclaiming liability for such events. Knowing the rules that govern this area is helpful and cost-effective.

Introduction to Real Property

THE CONCEPT OF FIXTURES

As mentioned above, real property is land and all things that attach. Fixtures are the "things that attach." Fixtures often start out as personal property but become real property when they attach to the land. Suppose, for example, that your hotel decides to install a refrigerator in each guest room. Before they are installed, the refrigerators are stored at a warehouse, where they are personal property. After they have been installed, the refrigerators become real property if they meet any one of the following "tests."

1. When removed, the fixture leaves a hole. If you install the refrigerators in the wall, when you remove them, there will be a hole. Under this test, the refrigerator has become so affixed to the real property that it has itself become real property.
2. The fixture changes the nature of the property. Did the refrigerators convert the room into a different room? Probably not. But screens and chairs might convert a room into a movie theater. If so, the personal property becomes real property.
3. The person attaching the fixture intends to make it a permanent attachment.

Proving that an item is a fixture does not require proof that all three tests have been met. Only one of the three tests must be proved.

THE IMPORTANCE OF FIXTURES

When personal property becomes attached to real property it becomes a part of the real property. As a result

- When the real property is sold, the fixture goes with it.
- The fixture is taxed as part of the real property.

When you buy or sell real estate be sure to designate in the sales contract any items that you will not consider as fixtures. For example, certain light fixtures that are attached to the property and would ordinarily be designated as fixtures may, by agreement of the parties, be removed. If you discuss this with the other party to the agreement, you can clarify from the earliest stages of negotiating the sale or purchase which fixtures stay with the property and which go.

FIXTURES IN A COMMERCIAL SETTING

In a commercial setting, special rules about fixtures apply. Suppose you rent space in a building for your restaurant. Since the purpose of the lease is for profit—to run a restaurant—it is deemed a commercial lease. Fixtures installed in this particular context *may* be removed when the commercial tenant leaves, so long as the tenant restores the property to its original condition. Thus, if you (a commercial tenant) install freezers in the storage room, any damage to floors and walls would have to be repaired. Note, however, that the rule allows you to take the freezers when you leave, despite the fact that they are fixtures.

Conveying Real Property

This section provides a limited discussion regarding the transference (conveying) of real property. The transfer is accomplished through a deed.

TYPES OF DEEDS

If you become involved in the sale or purchase of hotels and restaurants, a basic understanding of how land is transferred becomes important. (Notice that *land* is used synonymously with *real property* and that real property includes the buildings that are attached to it such as hotels and restaurants.)

Property is transferred, or conveyed, via a written document called a deed. The deed represents title to real property. Deeds generally come in the form of either a warranty deed or a quit claim deed.

A warranty deed contains covenants, or promises, about the title. These covenants guarantee the title's accuracy. A quit claim deed promises nothing. This deed conveys whatever interests the owner has in the property, if any. Thus, anyone could use a quit claim deed to convey property, regardless of his or her interest in the property.

PURCHASING REAL PROPERTY

If you purchase real property and you borrow money from the bank to pay for the land, several written documents are involved. In its simplest form, the sale would entail the following:

• The bank gives the buyer a check for the property
• The buyer gives the bank a note (promise to pay) and a mortgage (security for the note)
• The buyer then gives the seller the check for the property
• The seller gives the buyer a deed

Typically, the exchange of these items is called a closing.

The other major concern you would have in the sale or purchase of real property concerns title to the property. Title is a relatively complex subject that far exceeds the scope of this study guide. In essence, however, title is a measure of "time." The greatest estate is the fee simple. The fee simple represents title to real property that is infinite in duration. Any other title is a lesser estate. Therefore, the combination of a fee simple estate combined with a warranty deed may provide the best protection for the purchaser.

Personal Property

Chapters 15–18 of this study guide describe the liability of both innkeepers and restaurateurs for personal property. Personal property is all property other than real property and fixtures. Thus, your clothes, books, car, and furniture are all examples of personal property.

Bailments

An important concept in personal property is the bailment. The bailment relationship has special relevance to inns and restaurants.

BAILMENT DEFINED

A bailment is the transfer of personal property from the bailor to the bailee for a limited time and purpose, without the transfer of title. For example, a bailment occurs when you leave your clothes at the dry cleaners or leave your car at the service station for repairs.

The parties to the bailment are the bailor and the bailee. The bailor is the owner of the goods. The bailee is the person receiving the goods for a limited time and purpose.

CREATION OF THE BAILMENT

The bailment may be created expressly between the parties, or it may be implied by delivery and acceptance of the goods. No formal contract is needed, but the parties must consent to the creation of a bailment relationship.

The bailor must give up control over the property. Giving your car keys to the mechanic creates a bailment. Generally, parking your car in a garage and keeping the keys is not a bailment.

TYPES OF BAILMENTS

Mutual Benefit Bailment. If both the bailor and the bailee receive a benefit, a mutual benefit bailment exists. For example, the bailor gets her television fixed, and the bailee receives money. The bailee will be liable for ordinary negligence in this kind of bailment.

Bailment for the Benefit of the Bailor. In the second type of bailment, only the bailor benefits. For example, Millie watches Joe's dog while he is gone on business, and she receives no compensation. The bailee (Millie) is liable only for gross negligence, that is, negligence based on exceedingly reckless behavior.

Bailment for the Benefit of the Bailee. In the third type of bailment, only the bailee benefits. For example, Joe borrows Millie's lawn-mower for free. Millie is getting nothing in return. The bailee (Joe) is liable for the slightest negligence. Notice that the highest standard of care occurs here, and Joe has to exercise the greatest care over the property because only he is benefiting.

Constructive Bailment. If a guest leaves behind personal property in a restaurant or hotel, a constructive bailment is formed. The innkeeper (or restaurateur) has a legal duty of ordinary care and will be liable for ordinary negligence.

APPLICATION OF BAILMENTS TO THE HOSPITALITY INDUSTRY

An innkeeper forms a special bailment with guests when their personal property is relinquished to him or her. Bailments also have special application with regard to lost, misplaced, and abandoned property, which will be discussed in Chapter 15.

Review Questions for Chapter 14

Your answers to following questions should be based on rules and cases, not on opinion or facts.

1. Distinguish between real and personal property. What is the significance of the distinction? Describe a situation involving the sale of a hotel in which the distinction has legal ramifications. Be sure to use the appropriate tests for determining whether objects in your example are indeed fixtures.

2. Distinguish between private and commercial fixtures. What is the significance of the distinction?

3. Andrea made an offer to purchase a hotel for the amount of $2.9 million.

    a. Advise Andrea about what type of deed she should acquire and why.

    b. Advise Andrea about how title should be stated in the deed.

    c. Advise Andrea about whether the furniture in the hotel is included in the sale. You may assume that nothing was contained in the listing about the furniture.

4. The Fabulous Hotel has an underground parking garage. The Adams family arrives in a recreational vehicle, parks it, and takes the keys with them.

    a. What is the liability of the Fabulous Hotel when all the contents of the RV are stolen?

    b. Assume Mrs. Adams gave the key to the Fabulous Hotel's garage employee and the contents were stolen. Does the hotel have a different level of liability?

    c. What legal theory distinguishes these two examples?

5. Assume that the Adams family parked their RV in the Fabulous Hotel's underground parking garage and gave the keys to the garage attendant.

    a. Their son Brian's CD collection, concealed in a rear storage area of the RV, was stolen. Would the Fabulous Hotel have liability for this loss?

    b. Suppose that when the Adams gave the keys to the attendant, they received in exchange a parking stub that said, "The Fabulous is not liable for the loss of or damage to vehicles parked in this garage." What is the effect of this exculpatory clause? Is it valid?

CHAPTER 15

Innkeeper's Responsibility
for Property of Guests

I. Rules pertaining to liability for personal property.
   A. This chapter deals with the innkeeper's liability when personal property of a guest is damaged, destroyed, stolen, or lost.
   B. The law concerning an innkeeper's liability is not uniform throughout the United States; each state has its own laws regarding an innkeeper's liability.
   C. Therefore, in arriving at what an innkeeper's liability is, we will consider common-law *majority* rule, common-law *minority* rule, and statutory rules.
II. Common-law liability rules (12:1–12:2).
   A. General rule: common-law majority rule.
      1. More than twenty-five states (a majority) in the United States follow this rule. It was established in "Old England" by means of court decisions (thus, it is common law).
      2. The innkeeper is liable for goods *infra hospitium* ("within the confines of the inn"). This liability applies even if the innkeeper is *not* negligent and the loss is caused by such events as fire, theft, or burglary. This is called the rule of insurer's liability. To recover, all the guest has to prove is that his or her goods were lost while at the inn.
   B. Common-law minority rule (12:3).
      1. Fewer than twenty-five states (a minority) in the United States

follow this rule. It was also established through English law and court decisions.

2. The innkeeper is liable for goods *infra hospitium* only if the innkeeper is proven to be negligent. The innkeeper has the burden of proving that the loss did not occur through his or her negligence.

III. Statutory rules.

    A. Many state legislatures have superseded the "old law" (common law) by passing statutes limiting an innkeeper's liability for loss or damage to goods. Thus, even when the rules talk about absolute liability, you need to check that state's statutes to see whether the common law is still followed.

IV. Establishing the liability of the innkeeper.

    A. The following are common-law rules of liability. But remember as you read these that most states have superseded these rules with statutes that limit liability.

    B. Prior to the innkeeper-guest relationship (12:4).

        1. The innkeeper is liable for the loss of property if the person does in fact become a guest, but if the person never intended to become a guest, then there is no liability.

    C. Property in transit or when a third party delivers a guest's property to the inn (12:5–12:6).

        1. When an innkeeper maintained a system for the transportation of baggage for which a charge was made, and the claim check was delivered by the guest to the hotel, who delivered it to a series of transfer agents, the hotel was liable for the lost luggage in *Davidson v. Madison Corp.* (textbook, pp. 419–20).

        2. When the innkeeper-guest relationship had terminated, but the guests left instructions for property arriving after their departure, the hotel was liable for the loss of the package in *Berlow v. Sheraton Dallas Corp.* (textbook, pp. 421–25).

    D. Goods brought into the inn (12:7–12:8).

        1. The innkeeper is not necessarily liable for property brought

into the inn after arrival that is not in the "character of a guest." *Mateer v. Brown* (textbook, pp. 427–28).

2. The innkeeper is not liable for merchandise brought into the inn for sale or display (by a salesman with goods to sell). *Myers v. Cottrill* (textbook, pp. 426–27).

E. Property deposited in hotel lobby (12:9).

1. The innkeeper may be liable for property left in the appropriate place for check-in if the person ultimately becomes a guest. *Swanner v. Conner Hotel Co.* (textbook, pp. 428–29).

2. But if an employee of the inn gives directions contrary to posted regulations of the inn, the posted regulations prevail. *Widen v. Warren Hotel Co.* (textbook, pp. 429–30).

F. When fire causes loss (12:11).

1. As a general rule, the innkeeper is liable for any loss caused by fire, but can rebut evidence by a showing that he or she was not negligent. Compliance with the fire code is the minimum standard. *Herberg v. Swartz* (textbook, pp. 433–37).

G. When theft causes loss (12:12).

1. As a general rule, if a guest's property is stolen by an employee, the innkeeper is liable. If the property is stolen by a stranger, the innkeeper may also be liable. Many states have put a limit on how much the innkeeper will be liable for.

H. Loss in restaurant (12:15).

1. "One who is merely a customer at a bar, restaurant, barbershop . . . does not thereby establish the relationship of innkeeper and guest" (textbook, p. 124). Thus the loss of luggage checked with a hotel bellman while the owner was eating lunch at the hotel's restaurant could not be pursued under the *infra hospitium* theory in *Blakemore v. Coleman* (textbook, p. 444–48).

V. Automobiles (12:13).

A. Automobiles are a special problem.

1. The innkeeper is liable for goods brought into the inn (*infra hospitium*) and automobiles are not brought *into* the inn.

2. The scope of *infra hospitium* is changing in some states, however, and may include loss to a guest's property contained as far away from the hotel as the parking lot. *Aria v. Bridge House Hotel (Staines) Ltd.* (textbook, p. 438).
3. The theory was even applied to a local resident, not a guest, who parked in the inn's free parking space in *Williams v. Linnitt* (textbook, pp. 438–39).

B. Theories of liability for automobiles (12:13, 12:14).
1. Bailment and *infra hospitium*.
   a) A majority of states follow a theory of liability for cars based on bailments. For a bailment to be created the guest must give up the car keys, and the inn must agree to take possession.
   b) In *Governor House v. Schmidt* (textbook, pp. 440–42), a car was held to be *infra hospitium* and the hotel was held liable for the loss of plaintiff's car even though the garage was owned by a separate entity, because it appeared that the garage was part of the hotel.
   c) In *Shepherd Fleet, Inc. v. Opryland USA, Inc.* (textbook, pp. 442–44), plaintiff's car was deemed *infra hospitium*, and the hotel was held liable for damage when plaintiff turned her car and keys over to a hotel employee, who then parked the car adjacent to the hotel.
2. Insurer's liability for automobiles—minority rule (12:14).
   a) Adopted in only two states: Utah and Oklahoma.
   b) Under this theory the innkeeper is liable for the car and its contents even if he or she has no notice that the car is there. No elements of a bailment are necessary to establish liability.

C. Parking-lot transactions (12:16).
1. The innkeeper was held to be a "professional bailee" and could not therefore limit his liability by use of a disclaimer on a ticket in *Ellerman v. Atlanta American Motor Hotel Corp.* (textbook, pp. 448–49).
2. Some courts reject the bailment theory as the basis of lia-

bility, basing liability, instead, upon either "reasonable care under the circumstances whereby foreseeability shall be a measure of liability" (*Garlock v. Multiple Parking Services, Inc.*; textbook, pp. 449–52) or just "foreseeability" (*Danielenko v. Kinney Rent A Car, Inc.*; textbook, pp. 452–53).

D. Liability for goods left in the car (12:17).

    1. The hidden container rule. As a general rule, under bailments, the bailee is liable for goods about which he or she "knew or should have known." For example, the presence of a car stereo is visible, thus placing the bailee on notice of its presence. But if the goods are not visible, and the bailee is not told of their presence, then the bailee will not, as a general rule, be liable for their loss.

    2. The *infra hospitium* rule.

        a) If the automobile is *infra hospitium*, however, the hidden container rule does not apply. The innkeeper is liable for all the goods in the car whether hidden or not.

        b) An innkeeper was held liable for a truck, trailer, and contents stolen from the motel parking lot because the property was under the care of the innkeeper in *Vilella v. Sabine, Inc.* (textbook, pp. 454–57).

E. Apparent authority of employees for automobiles (12:18).

    1. Generally, an employee's statement of assurance given to a guest concerning the safety of goods binds the hotel.

    2. A statement by the porter to a guest that the contents of her car would be "safe" was held not to bind the hotel in *Brown v. Christopher Inn Co.* (textbook, pp. 458–59).

F. Disclaimers of liability (12:20–12:21).

    1. As a general rule, the courts will not enforce a disclaimer.

    2. Check the state's law to see whether disclaimers are void or enforceable. New York makes such a disclaimer void.

VI. Lost, misplaced, and abandoned property (12:22–12:25).

A. Acquiring title to lost, misplaced, or abandoned property—common-law rules.

    1. Lost property.

a) Property that was unintentionally placed and the owner cannot remember where it was left.

b) Title is always in the owner. If the owner never shows up, title goes to the *finder* of the property.

c) Under this rule, if an employee of the hotel finds a guest's wallet, and the guest never claims it, the employee acquires title. Most innkeepers have employees sign an agreement that all property found on the premises belongs to the inn to avoid disputes over whether the property was lost or misplaced (and thus over title to it).

2. Misplaced property.

a) Property that was intentionally placed and the owner cannot remember where it was placed.

b) Title is always in the owner. If the owner does not show up, title goes to the owner of the property where the misplaced item was found.

c) This rule makes sure that the true owner has the best chance of retracing his or her steps and finding the article. The owner of the property where the item is found must protect the item.

d) In *Jackson v. Steinberg* (textbook, pp. 466–68), $800, neatly stacked inside a drawer liner and discovered by a maid, was held to be misplaced property and therefore rightfully belonging to the inn, not the maid, when the true owner failed to show up.

3. Abandoned property.

a) Property that is intentionally given up.

b) Any finder may claim abandoned property, and the original owner may not reclaim it.

c) The finder must make sure the property is truly abandoned, or he or she may be liable for unlawfully taking the property.

d) Money left under a hotel's carpet for some fifteen years and then found by a contractor installing new carpet was held to be abandoned property in *Erickson v. Sinykin* (text-book, pp. 468–70).

   B. Acquiring title to lost, misplaced, or abandoned property—statu-tory rules (12:23–12:24).

      1. In New York State, if the property is worth more than $10, the finder must give it to the rightful owner or, if the owner can't be found, to the police. After a certain time, if the prop-erty goes unclaimed, the finder gets title.

      2. New York General Business Law section 217 provides that property not claimed by anyone within six months may be sold at a public auction.

Review Questions for Chapter 15 and Textbook, Chapter 12

Your answers to the following questions should be based on rules and cases, not on opinion or facts.

1. The Drew family arrives at the Rustic Motel in a large recre-ational vehicle stocked with personal belongings. Mrs. Drew enters the motel and registers the family for the night. She asks the front desk staff where there is a safe place to park the RV and explains that there are many articles of value inside it. What is the liability of the innkeeper when:

   a. The front desk staff directs the Drews to park the RV in the inn's parking lot, and all the contents of the RV are stolen dur-ing the night?

   b. A bellhop in the hotel directs the Drews where to park?

   c. There are many precious goods inside the RV, including jewels, which the Drews did not inform the staff of?

2. While Midge the maid is cleaning Room 110 she discovers a diamond ring on the edge of the bathtub, a fur coat still hanging in the closet, and thousand-dollar bills neatly stacked in a drawer in the

desk. Assume the rightful owner never shows up to claim any of this property.

   a. What steps should the hotel take before an incident like this occurs?

   b. What steps should the hotel take with regard to the found property?

   c. What is the hotel's liability for the goods?

   d. For each type of property found, determine who is the rightful owner—the maid or the hotel. Discuss, assuming a hotel policy exists and assuming one does not exist.

   3. Smedley enters the Fabulous Hotel intending to register as a guest. Distracted by a television program playing in the lobby, he sits down and becomes engrossed to the point that he fails to see a thief taking off with his briefcase and luggage.

   a. What, if any, liability does the hotel have for this incident?

   b. What difference does it make whether Smedley intends to register as a guest?

   c. Suppose Smedley is at the hotel merely to eat at the hotel's restaurant. Is the hotel liable for the loss?

CHAPTER 16

Exceptions and Limitations to Liability for Guest's Property

I. Common-law liability.
    A. Under the common law, the innkeeper is liable for the property
       of guests, *except* when the loss of property is due to:
       1. The neglect or fault of the guest (contributory negligence).
       2. An act of God.
       3. The act of a Public Enemy.
       4. Limitation by statute.
II. Exceptions to common-law liability.
    A. Contributory negligence of the guest (13:1–13:2).
       1. Failure to lock the door (13:3).
          a) If a guest's failure to lock the door contributed to the loss
             of personal property, the innkeeper is not liable.
          b) In *Cohen v. Janlee Hotel Corp.* (textbook, pp. 473–74), a
             guest went to bed and left the door unlocked to allow her
             roommate to come in. When she awoke, her Persian lamb
             coat was gone. The court held that she acted in a manner
             that facilitated the theft; therefore, the innkeeper was not
             liable.
       2. Failure to deliver valuables to the innkeeper (13:4).
          a) If the inn has posted signs that goods must be deposited
             and a guest fails to comply, the innkeeper is not liable.
          b) If a guest leaves valuables with the innkeeper in a public

room (this means left with permission of the innkeeper), the innkeeper is liable for the loss.
3. Publicly exhibiting money or valuables (13:6).
   a) The jury must decide if this constitutes contributory negligence, since it depends on the circumstances.
4. Intoxication (13:7).
   a) If a guest's condition contributes to the loss of property— i.e., too drunk to lock the door—and burglary follows, that constitutes contributory negligence. But if the loss is due to the negligence of the innkeeper, the innkeeper is liable. *Cunningham v. Bucky* (textbook, pp. 476–77).
B. Act of God (13:8).
   1. An occurrence that is unpredictable, such as a flood, tornado, frost, rain, or snow is considered an act of God.
   2. An act of God is a defense *if* there was no human intervention.
      a) For example, a tornado devastates a hotel, and all property is lost. The innkeeper is not liable. This is an act of God.
      b) In *Wolf Hotel Co. v. Parker* (textbook, pp. 477–78), the defendant innkeeper placed the plaintiff's luggage in a storage room, which then was flooded. The innkeeper was liable because the human intervention—placing the bags in the closet—mixed a human action with an act of God.
C. The act of a Public Enemy.
   1. The act of a country at war with the United States, *not* that of a criminal.
      a) *See Johnston v. Mobile Hotel Co.* (textbook, p. 479) for an example of an attempt to incorrectly apply the rule.
      b) Invasion of a hotel by a terrorist from a country with whom the United States is at war would be an act of a Public Enemy. The hotel is not liable for damage to personal property resulting from the invasion.
III. Statutory limitations of liability (13:10).

A. Under the theory of *infra hospitium*, the innkeeper is liable for the loss of a guest's property if none of the above exceptions apply, even if he or she was not negligent.

B. Because this high standard of law could be expensive for an innkeeper, many states have passed legislation limiting an innkeeper's liability. The content of these statutes varies from state to state.

C. The innkeeper's liability depends on the kind of property involved. If it is small compass (can fit in a safe), one set of rules applies. If, however, the property is large, like a fur coat, other rules apply.

D. Statutes pertaining to valuables (property that could conveniently be left in a safe).

1. If the state has a statute limiting liability of innkeepers who provide a safe, and the guest *does not* deposit items of small compass in the safe, the innkeeper either is not liable or is liable for a statutory amount *if negligent*.

   a) A fails to deposit a diamond bracelet. The bracelet is stolen from A's room. By statute, in state X, the innkeeper has no liability; if the innkeeper was not negligent, the innkeeper owes nothing. But if the theft was due to the negligence of the innkeeper, the innkeeper is liable for a limited statutory amount.

   b) Same example in state Y. By statute in state Y, the innkeeper is liable only for the statutory amount. Negligence is not a factor. The innkeeper is liable for a limited statutory amount regardless, but no more.

   c) In *Pachinger v. MGM Grand Hotel* (textbook, p. 480), even though the plaintiff was *not a guest* of the hotel when he checked his bags and received a claim check—stating that the hotel assumed limited liability and that a safe deposit box was available for valuables—the hotel was liable only for the statutory amount of $750.

    d) In *Terry v. Linscott Hotel Corp.* (textbook, pp. 516–20), thieves stole jewelry from the plaintiff's hotel room. The court held that under Arizona law, the innkeeper's liability was limited to the statutory amount when guests failed to deposit property in the safe, *unless* the innkeeper was guilty of active misfeasance. The court held that failure of the innkeeper to provide adequate security was nonfeasance, or an omission to act, and not misfeasance.

    e) In *Levitt v. Desert Palace, Inc.* (textbook, pp. 520–24), the hotel was held not liable for the theft of $1,300,000 worth of jewelry from a hotel room because the plaintiffs failed to show *gross* negligence on the part of the hotel, as required by Nevada statute.

2. If the state has a statute limiting liability of innkeepers who provide a safe, and the guest *does* use the safe deposit box or safe:

    a) The innkeeper may be liable for nothing.

    b) The innkeeper is liable only for the statutory amount if the loss is due to his or her negligence.

    c) In some states the innkeeper may be liable for more than the statutory amount if found grossly negligent.

    d) The innkeeper is liable for the full value of the property if the innkeeper did not properly post notices or failed to provide an adequate safe.

3. If the state does not have a statute limiting liability the innkeeper *may be* liable for the full value of the property (*infra hospitium* or bailment theories).

4. Contractual limitations of liability (13:13).

    a) In general, a hotel's attempt to limit (lessen) liability by contracting with the guest is not enforceable. *Oklahoma City Hotel v. Levine* (textbook, pp. 485–86).

5. Necessity of complying with the statute (13:14, 13:16, 13:17).

    a) Before the statute limiting liability is available, the innkeeper must comply with all parts of the statute. *Frockt v. Goodloc* (textbook, p. 486).

b) In New York, this includes:

   (1) Providing a safe. — but not the type of safe —
   (2) Posting—in a conspicuous manner, in a public place and in the office—a notice stating that the safe is available for the deposit of valuables and that the innkeeper's liability is limited (13:17).

6. Examples of failure to comply with statutes.

   a) In *Zaldin v. Concord Hotel* (textbook, pp. 487–90), the court held the innkeeper liable for the full amount because the guest did not have access to the safe between the hours of 11 P.M. and 8 A.M. Therefore, a safe was "not provided." If a safe is not provided, the innkeeper cannot limit his or her liability under the statute.

   b) In *Goncalves v. Regent International Hotels, Ltd.* (textbook, pp. 491–97), the court questioned whether a safe was even provided to guests because the safety deposit boxes were housed in a room built out of plasterboard, with ordinary tumbler locks and hollow doors.

   c) In *Depaemelaere v. Davis* (textbook, pp. 499–502), the plaintiff deposited $26,000 in a hotel's safe deposit box. When the box was opened, $10,000 was missing. The court held that the innkeeper was liable because the notices failed to state that depositing the money in the hotel's safe deposit boxes limited the innkeeper's liability to the statutory sum of $500.

   d) In *Carlton v. Beacon Hotel Corp.* (textbook, pp. 511–13), the plaintiff delivered $23,000 worth of jewelry to the desk clerk for deposit in a safe deposit box and the jewelry disappeared. The court held that the hotel was liable only for the statutory amount of $500 because the hotel provided a safe and posted notices.

absence of stated value and written agreement

   e) In *Kalpakian v. Oklahoma Sheraton Corp.* (textbook, pp.

[handwritten margin note: must advise owner to set more]

513–15), plaintiffs deposited $286,546, which then disappeared. The hotel's liability was limited to $1500 because of notice on the deposit boxes.

f) In *Zacharia v. Harbor Island Spa, Inc.* (textbook, pp. 509–11), the court held that an innkeeper did not have limited liability when the notice to guests was crossed off the card that accompanied their deposits and no receipt was given for the items, as required by Florida statute.

7. Articles required to be deposited in safe (13:18).

a) By statute, for example in New York State, the guest is *required* to deposit items of small compass, such as money, jewels, ornaments, securities, and stones.

b) Motor vehicles and trailers are not items of small compass. *Martin v. Holiday Inns, Inc.* (textbook, p. 503).

8. Watches (13:19).

a) In New York, watches are the type of property "useful or necessary to the comfort of the guest" and therefore do not need to be deposited in the safe. Other property falling into this category includes pens and pencils, rosaries, chains, and purses (13:20).

b) In other states, however, such articles must be deposited.

(1) In *Walls v. Cosmopolitan Hotels, Inc.* (textbook, pp. 504–5), the hotel was not liable for the loss of plaintiff's watch because he failed to deposit it in the safe.

(2) In *Brewer v. Roosevelt Motor Lodge* (textbook, pp. 506–9), plaintiff's watch was held not to be jewelry or a personal ornament. Thus the innkeeper was a "depository for hire" by statute and plaintiff could collect only $50.

9. Gambling casino safes (13:23).

a) Where gambling is legal, the common mode of conduct when depositing money in the hotel safe is for the innkeeper to mark the amount of money on deposit and thereby assume liability for the full amount.

10. Loss due to theft by employees (13:24).

a) As a general rule, an employee who commits a crime is "outside the scope of employment" and therefore the inn is not liable *beyond* the statutory amount for the theft. *Millhiser v. Beau Site Co.* (textbook, pp. 526–7).

11. Delivery of property to an employee of the inn (13:26).

a) If the goods are *infra hospitium*, the innkeeper is liable under a general common-law rule (bailment) and *respondeat superior*.

b) In *Spiller v. Barclay Hotel* (textbook, pp. 529–30), a guest turned her bags over to a bellhop to watch as she checked out, and subsequently one of the bags was missing. The innkeeper was held liable for the negligence of its employee. This included liability for the loss of jewelry—for its full value—since plaintiff was in the process of checking out and could not be expected to use the safe.

12. Waiver of statutory limitation (13:29).

a) In any situation in which the innkeeper accepts a guest's property, the innkeeper may become liable for the full value of the goods *by agreement*. Thus, when depositing jewels, the guest may request additional coverage, to which the inn may or may not agree. If the inn does not agree, of course, liability is limited to the statutory amount.

b) An employee's suggestion to a guest that she deposit her jewelry in the hotel's safe deposit boxes does not waive the statute; the hotel still has limited liability. *Mitsuya v. Croydon Management Co.* (textbook, pp. 531–32).

E. Statutory limitations for property other than valuables (13:30).

1. Loss of property other than valuables from rooms may carry a statutory limitation in some states. In New York, the innkeeper is liable for the full value if the innkeeper was negligent.

a) In *DeBanfield v. Hilton Hotels Corp.* (textbook, p. 535), the guest failed to prove the innkeeper negligent for the theft of luggage from his room and therefore was limited to the statutory amount of $500 for the loss.

b) In *Bhattal v. Grand Hyatt–New York* (textbook, pp. 538–41), when a hotel inadvertently transferred a guest's luggage from New York City to Saudi Arabia, the innkeeper was held liable for the full amount including jewels contained therein.

2. Loss of property from places other than rooms (checkrooms, lobby) is limited to the amount declared on the claim check. To recover in excess of the statute, a guest would have to either declare a higher amount on the claim check or prove negligence of the innkeeper (13:30).

Review Questions for Chapter 16 and Textbook, Chapter 13

Your answers to the following questions should be based on rules and cases, not on opinion or facts.

1. The Brookers made a reservation to stay at the Fabulous Hotel for their wedding anniversary during a weekend in April. When they arrived, the hotel stored their luggage in a storage room and gave the Brookers a claim check that by its terms limited the hotel's liability to the statutory sum of $50. What is the hotel's liability in each of the following situations?

a. When the Brookers return to the hotel, their luggage is gone.

b. The Brookers tell the clerk at the storage room that the value of the property in the luggage is $2000. The clerk says "Don't worry. I'll keep an eye on it and make sure nothing happens."

c. There is a flood that afternoon in the city where the hotel is located. It destroys all property on the first floor of the hotel including the Brookers' luggage.

d. A thief steals the Brookers' luggage from the storeroom.

e. The hotel accidentally ships out the luggage with other luggage stored. The Brookers' luggage is never found. Jewels valued at $25,000 are lost.

2. The Merriweathers own an enormous amount of jewelry. Assume the following events occur after they check into the Ritzy Hotel.

a. They deposit the jewels, worth $2,000,000, in the safe deposit box. The jewels are stolen from the hotel. Assume that the state in which the Ritzy is located has a statute limiting liability to $500. What is the hotel's liability?

b. What is the effect if the hotel never posted signs saying that the boxes were available for rental?

c. What is the effect if the hotel's negligence caused the theft?

d. Suppose the jewels were in the Merriweathers' room and not in the safe deposit box. What is the hotel's liability if the gems are stolen from their room?

* N.Y. General Bus Law
Sections 200 +

CHAPTER 17

Innkeeper's Duty to Nonguests

I. Common-law duties to nonguests, in general.
 A. No duty to admit nonguests (14:1). But one who is neither a guest nor a person having business with a guest may enter to make an inquiry (14:8).
 B. Nonguests have access to inn to visit guests of inn (14:2–14:3). But nonguests engaged in illegal activity, such as prostitution, have no right of access to the inn. *Kelly v. United States* (textbook, pp. 549–51).
 C. Nonguests have access to do business with guests (14:4), but innkeeper may exclude those soliciting business (14:5). With regard to travel-related businesses, an innkeeper who admits one common carrier may not exclude others (14:6).
II. Common-law responsibility for property of nonguest.
 A. As a general rule, there is no innkeeper liability for the loss of property belonging to nonguests, unless the innkeeper is negligent (14:9).
 B. In *Jacobs v. Alrae Hotel Corp.* (textbook, pp. 553–56), an innkeeper was not held liable when jewels owned by a tenant (nonguest) of the hotel were stolen from a safe deposit box at the hotel because the standard of care is that of merely a warehouseman.
 C. But in *Wallinga v. Johnson* (textbook, pp. 556–58), an innkeeper was held subject to a bailment standard for the theft of plaintiff's rings from the hotel safe, even though plaintiff was not a guest

but a tenant (nonguest). These two cases illustrate different outcomes arising from different judges and courts.

D. A hotel was held liable under a bailment theory for the loss of a tenant's (nonguest's) trunks in *Dalton v. Hamilton Hotel Operating Co.* (textbook, pp. 558–61).

E. Whether an innkeeper is liable for the loss of a nonguests' property, when it is accepted by an employee, depends on whether the employee had the authority to accept the property (14:12).

F. The innkeeper is liable for delivering a nonguest's property to the wrong person (14:13).

Review Questions for Chapter 17 and Textbook, Chapter 14

Your answers to the following questions should be based on rules and cases, not on opinion or facts.

1. You are the night desk clerk at the Average Hotel. One evening you are going about your duties, which include deciding whether you have a duty to admit the following people to the inn. State a rule, not opinion, that supports your position.

 a. A local political organization would like to conduct a poll in the lobby.

 b. The Girl Scouts wish to go door-to-door to sell cookies to guests.

 c. A masseuse wants to enter to give a guest a backrub.

 d. A local barber wishes to set up shop.

 e. A local airport limousine service wishes to set up shop.

2. Still continuing in your position in question 1 above, state the liability of the Average Hotel for the following:

 a. A "lobby lizard" cannot find a pair of gloves that he thinks he left in the hotel that evening.

 b. The masseuse mentioned above has lost her purse at the hotel.

 c. A tenant's (nonguest) jewels are stolen from the safe.

Responsibility of Restaurant Keeper for Patron's Property

I.   Liability of the restaurateur for loss of property.
   A. Restaurants differ from inns (15:1).
      1. In *Augustine v. Marriott Hotel* (textbook, pp. 564–65), an innkeeper had *no* duty to a seminar attendee whose coat was stolen from a rack outside the seminar room at the hotel. The person was not a guest, and there was no bailment.
   B. For the restaurateur to be liable, the patron must prove either a bailment or negligence.
      1. Bailments (15:2).
         a) If the restaurant accepts custody of the patron's property, the restaurant will be liable for its loss, as an express bailment.
         b) If the restaurant does not accept custody of the property, but the property is placed somewhere at the direction of the restaurateur, there may be an implied bailment.
      2. Negligence.
         a) In *Shamrock Hilton Hotel v. Caranas* (textbook, pp. 574–77), the hotel restaurant was found negligent when a busboy gave a patron's misplaced purse to the cashier, who then surrendered it to the wrong person. The hotel was not entitled to statutory limitation protection.

[150]

C. When is the restaurant not liable?
1. In *Wentworth v. Riggs* (textbook, pp. 566–68), there was no bailment for a coat left on a hook.
2. In *Black Bert Lounge and Restaurant v. Meisnere* (textbook, pp. 568–69), there was no bailment for a coat hung in a cloakroom at the direction of a waitress.
3. In *Wielar v. Silver Standard, Inc.* (textbook, pp. 571–72), there was no bailment for an overcoat hung in a self-serve cafeteria.
4. In *Montgomery v. Ladjing* (textbook, pp. 572–74), the restaurant was not liable for a coat on a hook near the table, because no notice was given to the restaurant of the coat's presence and there was no proof of negligent supervision of the premises.

II. Liability for damage to property.
A. In *Block v. Sherry* (textbook, p. 574), spilling water on patron was held to be negligence.

III. Statutory liability (15:7).
A. Many states have a statute limiting a restaurant keeper's liability. For example, the following list illustrates application of New York statutes to different situations.
1. If the restaurant takes control of the coat, and the guest does not state a value, maximum liability is $200.
2. In *Weinberg II* (textbook, pp. 578–83), New York's limitation of liability (then $75) was held to apply to the loss of a checked $7500-coat that was lost by the restaurant.
3. If the guest *does* state a value and receives a receipt, maximum liability is $300, regardless of the value of the item, unless the restaurant keeper is negligent (textbook, p. 583).
4. If the restaurant *charges* to store the item, and negligence of the restaurant causes the loss, the restaurant is liable for the full value of the item.
5. The limitation of liability does not apply to discotheques. Studio 54 was held liable on the bailment theory for the loss of a

$1250 leather coat. *Conboy v. Studio 54, Inc.* (textbook, pp. 584–86).

B. Many restaurants post a notice limiting their liability.
   1. As a general rule in New York State such a posting has no effect unless the restaurant can prove that the patron saw the notice and consented to the limitation. *Conboy, supra*.
   2. New York prohibits hotels, motels, or restaurants from disclaiming or misrepresenting liability.

Review Questions for Chapter 18 and Textbook, Chapter 15

Your answers to the following questions should be based on rules and cases, not on opinion or facts.

1. Jeeves enters the Fancy Restaurant for lunch. Discuss the liability of the restaurant for the following incidents. In all cases, the coat is missing after Jeeves finishes his lunch.
   a. Jeeves places his coat on a hook.
   b. A waiter tells Jeeves to place his coat on a hook.
   c. Jeeves leaves his coat in the unattended coatroom.
   d. Jeeves checks his coat with an employee at the coatroom, and the employee receives a tip.
   e. Jeeves checks his coat with an employee at the coatroom, and the employee receives no payment.
   f. Jeeves checks his coat with an employee at the coatroom who receives $2 for each coat checked.

P A R T   V

GOVERNMENT REGULATION OF THE HOSPITALITY INDUSTRY

CHAPTER 19

Franchise Agreements:
Legal Rights and Responsibilities
of Franchisor and Franchisee

I. Franchise (17:1).
   A. An agreement in which the franchisee obtains the right to use the franchisor's trademark, tradename, or copyright in purveying goods or services.
   B. Subject to regulation by the Federal Trade Commission.
II. The franchise agreement (17:2).
   A. In general, the franchisee agrees to free the franchisor from liability for the negligence of the franchisee; to be an independent contractor; and to be primarily liable for contracts with third parties (17:3).
III. Liability of the franchisor for acts of the franchisee (17:4).
   A. The franchisor may be liable to a third party if the third party can show that the franchisor had "sufficient control" over the franchisee.
   B. The theory of liability is a principal-agency relationship, where the principal is the franchisor and the agency is the franchisee. Liability lies with the agency.
   C. The principal will be liable for the agent's actions if:
      1. The principal has control over the actions of the agent. In *Sapp v. City of Tallahassee* (textbook, pp. 617–19), the court considered Holiday Inn's control over its franchisee to deter-

[155]

mine liability, despite a franchise agreement expressly stating
that the franchisor was not in a principal-agency relationship.

2. The principal made it look to a third party as if the agent had
the authority to act on the principal's behalf. This is called
apparent authority or authority by estoppel (17:5). *Crinkley v.
Holiday Inns, Inc.* (textbook, pp. 619–21).

IV. Contractual disclaimers of liability (17:6).

    A. Suggestions for franchisor to avoid liability: conspicuous notice
or legislation, or both.

Review Questions for Chapter 19 and Textbook, Chapter 17

Your answers to the following questions should be based on rules
and cases, not on opinion or facts.

1. Patricia Langley owns a large real estate concern, Langley Properties. Bob Francis would like to use Patricia's business name, with
her permission, and seeks your advice on how to apply for and obtain
a franchise. Briefly outline what you will tell him.

2. Allie, one of Patricia's agents, currently owns a franchise for
Langley Properties. Last week, Allie was showing a client a specific
property when the automobile they were in was in an accident. Both
Allie and the prospective client were seriously injured.

    a. Discuss the likely outcome of a lawsuit by Allie against Langley
Properties and Patricia Langley.

    b. Discuss the likely outcome of a lawsuit by the client against
Langley Properties and against Patricia Langley and Allie.

    c. Would it make any difference if Patricia had introduced Allie to
the client by stating, "This is my agent Allie. She will take good
care of you and report back to me."

CHAPTER 20

Regulation Governing the Sale of Food, Beverages, and Intoxicants

I. Federal regulation of food and beverages (18:1).
    A. The Food and Drug Administration is the federal administrative agency that oversees violations of the Food, Drug and Cosmetic Act (18:1, 18:2).
    B. The Food, Drug and Cosmetic Act (FDCA).
        1. Prohibits products harmful to the consuming public and misrepresentation.
        2. Requires disclosure of information when products are sold.
    C. Violations of the Food, Drug and Cosmetic Act.
        1. *Adulteration* means food prepared, packed, or processed in such a way that it is contaminated with "filth" [§402(a) FDCA].
            a) In *Jean Pierre, Inc. v. State* (textbook, pp. 626–28), rodent feces, urine, and hair in and around flour sacks and cooking utensils supported accusations of adulteration.
        2. Economic adulteration is the use of cheaper ingredients, dilution, or concealment of the inferior nature of the product, amounting to consumer fraud (18:3).
        3. Misbranding of food (18:4).
            a) False labeling.
            b) Selling under the name of another food (must show intent to defraud).

[157]

          c) Packing in a misleading container (but if the defendant can show that the safety or cost-saving qualities of the container outweigh the deceptive aspects, that is an affirmative defense).

          d) Failure to prominently display information required by the FDCA.

    D. Enforcement of the FDCA. The Food and Drug Administration has the right to:

        1. Seize and destroy or sell misbranded or adulterated food (18:5).

        2. Issue an injunction (18:7).

        3. Issue a citation for a misdemeanor (18:6).

II. Federal regulation of advertising (18:8).

    A. The Federal Trade Commission (FTC).

        1. Prohibits misleading advertising of a material fact.

        2. The test for misleading advertising is whether the advertisement has the *tendency* or *capacity* to deceive.

    B. Enforcement.

        1. The FTC can enjoin the release of false advertisements.

        2. The FTC may require disclaimers in subsequent advertisements.

    C. Truth-in-menu legislation (18:10).

        1. A consumer movement to compel restaurants to be truthful with regard to representations made on their menus.

        2. Passed in a few states and cities.

        3. Examples of misrepresentation on menus.

          a) A misleading description of the quality or grade of the product.

          b) Stating an incorrect size or weight.

          c) Stating that foods are fresh when they are really frozen, canned, or preserved.

          d) Substituting another product for a brand-name product advertised.

          e) Substituting another type or cut of meat for the one advertised.

III. Federal regulation of smoking (18:11).
  A. There is no general *federal* law prohibiting smoking.
  B. Forty-two states have enacted legislation; some, like New York, require smoking and nonsmoking areas in restaurants serving more than fifty people.
  C. In *Gasper v. Louisiana Stadium and Exposition District* (textbook, pp. 640–43), a Louisiana suit to stop tobacco smoking in the Superdome, the court said there is no constitutional right that protects nonsmokers.
IV. Federal regulation of liquor. The U.S. Constitution permits alcohol consumption.
V. State regulation of liquor (18:14).
  A. Each state has a state liquor authority.
    1. All states require a liquor license in order to sell alcoholic beverages. This license is a privilege that may be revoked. Revocation of the license results in termination of the operation of the bar.
    2. A bar or restaurant obtains a liquor license by applying to the local liquor authority. If approved there, it is passed along to the state authority. This agency has "broad authority" to grant or deny the license; and may deny if there is some "rational reason."
    3. An applicant must be 21 years old, be a citizen of the United States, and have no felony convictions (certain misdemeanor convictions also prevent approval).
  B. Types of behavior regulated in establishments that serve liquor.
    1. Disorderly conduct: acts that tend to corrupt the morals of the community (18:15).
    2. Gambling that is continuous in nature, not including legalized gambling allowed in many states (18:16).
    3. Sexual misconduct.
      a) Prostitution makes premises subject to loss of its license (18:19). *Awrich Restaurant Inc. v. New York State Liquor Authority* (textbook, p. 655).
      b) Nudity is allowed in some states.

        c) Homosexual activity (18:18). In *One Eleven Wines & Liquors, Inc. v. Division of ABC* (textbook, pp. 650–54), the court stated that mere congregation of homosexuals is not "offensive to current standards of morality."

        d) Sexually explicit entertainment (18:20). In *Bellanca v. New York State Liquor Authority* (textbook, pp. 656–59), the court held that topless dancing is a protected "expression" under the First Amendment.

    4. Illegal activity (18:22). Drug trafficking is obviously illegal and will cause the revocation of a liquor license. *Collins v. State Liquor Authority* (textbook, pp. 667–69).

  C. Private clubs (18:21). For a private club to be exempt from New York Alcoholic Beverage Control Law, it cannot operate for a profit. *N.Y. State Liquor Authority v. Salem Social Club* (textbook, pp. 665–67).

Review Questions for Chapter 20 and Textbook, Chapter 18

Your answers to the following questions should be based on rules and cases, not on opinion or facts.

1. The Wild Bar and Restaurant, located in New York State, has a current, valid liquor license. The owners wish to introduce some exotic entertainment to increase business. Please advise them on the following:

    a. Could they qualify for a private club exemption?

    b. What would be the advantage of qualifying for this exemption?

    c. Could they have nude male and female dancers? Nude waiters and waitresses?

2. Annah has severe asthma and demands a nonsmoking seat in your restaurant. Assume you are located in New York State.

    a. Under what circumstances must you accommodate her request?

    b. Is there a federal law that Annah could use to her advantage?

3. Your restaurant (in New York State) wishes to advertise on the local cable channel.

    a. What is the standard imposed by the law with regard to the "truth" of advertising?

    b. What law prevails?

4. Your restaurant also wishes to have the advertising firm design and produce a new menu. Assume you are located in New York.

    a. What standard is imposed?

    b. What law prevails?

5. Your manufacturing company produces a "health bread."

    a. With what standard of cleanliness in production must your factory comply?

    b. Which governmental agency regulates your plant?

CHAPTER 21

Responsibility Arising from
the Sale of Food, Beverages,
and Intoxicants

I. Innkeeper's liability for serving unfit or adulterated food (19:1).
    A. Negligence (failure to exercise reasonable care) is rarely used as
        a basis for recovery because noticeably spoiled food is rarely
        served (19:1).
    B. Breach of implied warranty of merchantability (19:2).
        1. The goods must be sold by a merchant.
        2. The warranty does not have to be stated.
        3. The goods must be "fit for the ordinary purposes for which
            such goods are used" (Uniform Commercial Code).
        4. In *Averitt v. Southland Motor Inn of Oklahoma* (textbook, pp.
            693–95), repeated violations of health code standards by per-
            mitting unsanitary conditions to exist was enough evidence to
            allow plaintiff to recover over $500,000 in punitive damages
            for exposure to shigella.
    C. Privity of contract (19:3).
        1. Traditionally recovery was limited to a plaintiff who had a
            contractual relationship with the seller.
        2. But in *Conklin v. Hotel Waldorf Astoria Corp.* (textbook, pp.
            674–76), a patron of a restaurant, who was injured when she
            bit into a roll containing glass, could recover even though she

did not pay for lunch and was not in direct privity with the hotel.

D. The foreign-natural test for determining what food is "fit for ordinary purposes" (19:4).

    1. In many states, if an item found in food is *natural* to the food then the food is not unwholesome. If, however, the item is *foreign* to the food, then the food will most likely be deemed adulterated, unmerchantable, or unwholesome.

    2. Natural.

        a) Chicken bone in a chicken pot pie. *Mix v. Ingersoll Candy Co.* (textbook, p. 680).

        b) Cherry stone in slice of cherry pie. *Musso v. Picadilly Cafeterias, Inc.*, (textbook, pp. 680–81).

        c) Fish bone in fish chowder. *Webster v. Blue Ship Tea Room, Inc.* (textbook, pp. 677–80).

    3. Foreign.

        a) Mass of material at bottom of bottle. *Miller v. Atlantic Bottling Corp.* (textbook, pp. 689–90).

        b) Glass in a roll. *Conklin v. Hotel Waldorf Astoria Corp.* (textbook, pp. 674–76).

        c) A pearl in oyster stew. *Matthews v. Campbell Soup Co.* (textbook, pp. 682–84).

II. Defenses to liability for serving unwholesome food.

A. Failure to prove proximate cause (19:5).

    1. If the plaintiff cannot show a direct connection between the adulterated food and the illness (proximate cause; see Chapter 11) then the plaintiff cannot prevail.

B. Opportunity to inspect (19:7).

    1. In some states, if the consumer has an opportunity to inspect the food before eating it, the seller is not liable if the unwholesomeness is noticeable.

    2. In other states, the consumer can recover on the basis of strict liability.

C. Assumption of the risk.

1. Assumption of the risk is a defense to torts and is usually seen in a high-risk context, such as sky diving, boxing, or skiing. It is unusual, but does occur, that assumption of the risk is a defense in the context of prepared food.
2. In *Hoch v. Venture Enterprises, Inc.* (textbook, pp. 691–93), the court said the jury could consider whether the plaintiffs assumed the risk of illness when they ate raw native hind fish and became ill.

III. Civil liability for illegal sale of liquor: Dram Shop Acts (19:9).

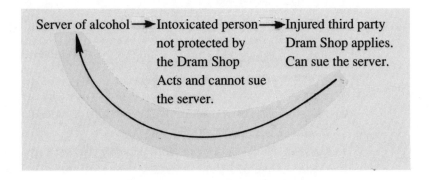

A. Overview (19:9).
   1. Deal with seller's liability for death of or injury to third parties as a result of his or her commercial establishment serving intoxicating beverages to a person apparently or actually under the influence of alcohol.
B. Under the common law, the server was not liable to the guest or to a third party injured as the result of the actions of the intoxicated guest.
C. Cases based on Dram Shop Acts.
   1. In *Mitchell v. The Shoals, Inc.* (textbook, pp. 705–6), a bartender served an inebriated guest, who drove the car in which plaintiff was injured. Plaintiff was herself seriously inebriated, but under New York State Dram Shop rules, that fact

   alone did not preclude her recovery, against the bar, for her
   injuries.

2. The New York State Dram Shop Act has no application to a
   private host in a private setting. Therefore, in *Kohler v. Wray*
   (textbook, pp. 712–15), a host who served beer at a party
   was not liable.

3. Hawaii also does not extend liability to social hosts. *Johnston
   v. KFC National Management Co.* (textbook, pp. 741–43).

4. But in New Jersey, a social host or other noncommercial provider of alcoholic beverages will be liable for injuries caused
   to third parties as the result of furnishing beverages to an
   obviously intoxicated person. *Coulter v. Superior Court* (textbook, pp. 696–99).

5. In Pennsylvania, a social host may be liable for serving intoxicating beverages to a person under twenty-one, but the social
   host may use contributory negligence as a defense. *Congini
   by Congini v. Portersville Valve Co.* (textbook, pp. 732–37).

6. In Connecticut, social hosts may be liable for wanton and
   reckless serving of alcohol that causes injury or death to a
   third party. *Kowal v. Hofher* (textbook, p. 737).

7. In *Matalavage v. Sadler* (textbook, pp. 709–12), a bar was
   held liable under the New York Dram Shop Act to the surviv-
   ing child of an intoxicated bar patron who was killed in an
   automobile accident.

8. In 1978, California abolished tort liability against the fur-
   nisher of alcoholic beverages except in one situation—providing alcohol to an obviously intoxicated minor. Therefore, in
   Hepe v. Paknad (textbook, pp. 715–19), plaintiff could not
   recover against a bar-restaurant for injuries resulting from the
   actions of an intoxicated patron of the bar.

IV. Defenses to the Dram Shop Acts (19:10).

   A. The plaintiff's own intoxication equals contributory negligence
   or assumption of the risk. *Williams v. Klemsrud* (textbook, pp.
   737–39).

V. Minors
    A. In a pre-1978 California ruling, a bartender's actions were
        deemed willful, and he could be held liable for the death of a
        "just turned 21 year-old" patron after serving him ten straight
        shots of rum, vodka collins, and beer chasers. *Ewing v. Clover-
        leaf Bowl* (textbook, pp. 721–25).
    B. In *Calendrino v. Shakey's Pizza Parlor Company, Inc.* (text-
        book, pp. 701–3), the California Dram Shop Act did not protect
        a minor who sued a server because he became intoxicated and
        then accepted a ride and was injured in an automobile accident.
    C. In Arizona, one who serves intoxicating liquors to a minor is
        liable both to third parties who might be injured as well as to the
        minor himself. *Brannigan v. Raybuck* (textbook, pp. 727–32).

Review Questions for Chapter 21 and Textbook, Chapter 19

Your answers to the following questions should be based on rules
and cases, not on opinion or facts.

1. The Hendersons went to dinner at the Atrocious Restaurant. During the meal the following events occurred. For each event, discuss
the liability of the restaurant to the Hendersons.
    a. While eating an oyster, Mrs. Henderson bit down on a pearl and
        cracked her tooth.
    b. Mr. Henderson ate dirt on his salad leaves. He now thinks it
        might have been the cause of his subsequent stomach distress,
        but he's not sure.
    c. Young Henderson sampled an exotic fish and, deciding he liked
        it, had a large plateful. The waiter warned him that some people
        cannot tolerate this especially hard-to-digest fish. The next day,
        he had an acute attack of bowel distress.
2. What are the Dram Shop Acts? What is their intended purpose?

3. The bartender at the Blitz Bar served Johnson ten drinks. Johnson became highly intoxicated, caused an automobile wreck, and injured Toledo.

   a. Advise Toledo on bringing a Dram Shop Act–based lawsuit in New York and in California. (Assume no jurisdiction issues; assume no minors.)
   b. May Johnson bring an action under the Dram Shop Acts for any injuries she sustained? Why?
   c. Would it make any difference if Johnson were a minor? Explain.

PART VI

INNKEEPER CREDITOR-DEBTOR PROTECTION

CHAPTER 2 2

The Innkeeper's Lien

I. The common-law lien (20:1–20:2).
   A. An innkeeper has the right to keep and sell a guest's personal property if the guest does not pay his or her bill.
   B. The lien applies to the goods in the inn as soon as the guest arrives (20:3–20:5).
   C. Lien does not apply to:
      1. Prior charges (20:4).
      2. Clothing on the guest's person (20:5).
      3. The guest himself (20:6).
      4. Property otherwise exempt (20:7).
      5. Goods of a third party if the innkeeper knows the goods are not the guest's (20:8).
      6. Goods of persons who are not responsible for the charges (20:9).
   D. The following acts do not affect the lien:
      1. Sale of goods by the owner to a third party (20:11).
      2. Removal of the property to another state (20:12).
   E. The lien is:
      1. Terminated by voluntary delivery of the goods to the guest (20:14), payment of the bill (20:17), conversion of the goods (20:18).
      2. Not terminated by fraud (20:15), temporary possession by the guest (20:16), or extension of time to pay (20:19).

II. The statutory lien (20:20).
   A. All states have a lien law that sets out how to take possession of goods, sell them, and collect the monies owed.
   B. In New York State, the guest whose property is seized is entitled to constitutional "due process" notice and the opportunity for a "hearing." *Blye v. Globe-Wernicke Realty Co.* (textbook, pp. 755–58).
   C. But in Illinois the seizure is not related to the state, therefore the guest has no constitutional protection. *Anastasia v. The Cosmopolitan National Bank of Chicago* (textbook, pp. 758–62).

CHAPTER 23

Compensation of the Innkeeper

I. Common-law rules.
   A. The innkeeper has a duty to charge reasonable rates (21:1).
   B. The innkeeper may charge lower rates to certain groups (clergy, armed services, or local residents). *Archibald v. Cinerama Hotels* (textbook, pp. 767–770).
   C. The innkeeper may fix rates (21:2).
   D. The innkeeper may charge a higher price if guest made an advance reservation (21:4).
II. Statutory and municipal rules.
   A. Rates must be posted in accordance with state rules (21:3).
   B. The innkeeper must abide by posted rules.
III. In general.
   A. The innkeeper has a right to get paid when a guest registers (21:5).
   B. Spouses of guests and parents of minors may be liable for charges furnished as "necessaries" (21:8).
   C. The innkeeper may enforce payment through the innkeeper's lien. (See Chapter 22 and textbook, Chapter 20.)

Review Questions for Chapters 22 and 23 and Textbook, Chapters 20 and 21

Your answers to the following questions should be based on rules and cases, not on opinion or facts. (For information on licensing, refer to Chapter 6.)

1. The Sloppy Hotel, located in New York State, is managed by Glenda Cooper. Glenda forgot to renew the Sloppy's state innkeeper license as well as the restaurant and liquor licenses on March 14. Ace registers at the Sloppy Hotel on March 15. Subsequently, Ace learns of the hotel's failure to file its license permits with the state. Discuss the legality of each of the following actions.
   a. Ace refuses to pay his hotel bill upon checking out, arguing that he is not liable because the hotel did not renew its hotel license.
   b. Ace refuses to pay his bar bill because the bar's license was not renewed.
   c. Ace refuses to pay his bar bill because the bartender's license was not renewed.
   d. Ace refuses to pay because he was charged more for his room than he felt was appropriate.
   e. Ace refuses to pay because he was charged more for his room than was paid by those staying at the hotel for a convention.
   f. Ace refuses to pay because the hotel failed to post its rates.
   g. Ace refuses to pay for his spouse or his children, claiming they are independently liable.

2. As a result of the Smith family's refusal to pay its bill, the Fabulous Hotel contemplates the following actions. For each example, state the rule of law and what advice, based on that rule, you would give the hotel.
   a. The hotel decides to let the Smiths stay in their room as long as they like, but to keep asking them for payment.
   b. The hotel decides to lock the Smiths out of their room, take all

their personal property, and sell it the next day at a sheriff's auction.

c. The hotel decides to lock the Smiths out, but to allow them to take all their personal property with them.

PART VII

SELECTED TOPICS

CHAPTER 24

Crimes against Innkeepers

I. Theft of services.
   A. Occurs when a guest leaves the hotel or restaurant without paying for services (22:1).
   B. The state must plead (in its charging papers) and prove that the defendant actually obtained the accommodations with the *intent* not to pay for lodging. *Agnew v. State* (textbook, pp. 776–77).
   C. Intent to defraud means that the defendant was "secretive, clandestine or surreptitious" in avoiding payment of the bill. *State v. Wagenius* (textbook, pp. 778–80).
   D. Mere failure to pay is not enough to prove guilt. The state must show that the accommodations were obtained by false or fictitious show of baggage; the defendant left the state without paying; the defendant gave a bad check; or the defendant surreptitiously removed his or her baggage. *Cottonreeder v. State* (textbook, pp. 782–84).
II. Defenses available.
   A. No intent to defraud. *State v. Kingsley* (textbook, pp. 785–86).
   B. No surreptitious activity (22:6).
   C. Tender of payment, even if a bad check. *People v. Dukatt* (textbook, p. 787).
   D. Malicious prosecution (22:8).
      1. If the innkeeper brings an unwarranted action against the de-

fendant and loses, the defendant may then sue the innkeeper for malicious prosecution.

2. Managers should be careful to seek competent legal advice before instituting any lawsuits. Otherwise, the potential for entanglement in a malicious prosecution lawsuit may exist, leading to, at the least, financial losses.

3. Under Puerto Rican law the standard is whether the hotel acted reasonably in pressing charges, not whether the evidence was sufficient to convict. In *Vince v. Posadas de Puerto Rico, S.A.* (textbook, pp. 789–92), a hotel notified police that two of its guests had failed to pay a substantial bill despite repeated demands by the hotel. The police investigated and arrested the plaintiffs, who eventually were acquitted. They then sued the hotel for malicious prosecution.

Review Questions for Chapter 24 and Textbook, Chapter 22

Your answers to the following questions should be based on rules and cases, not on opinion or facts.

1. Six fraternity brothers decided to enjoy the finer side of Florida during their spring break. Lacking money and credit cards, they hit on a scheme to check into the Oceanside Luxury Hotel and sneak out at the end of their vacation. After a week of fun in the sun, the brothers snuck out of the hotel at 3 A.M., leaving a bill of $2100. Assume that the fraternity brothers are located in a different state than the hotel.

a. Would you advise the hotel to bring a civil or criminal action or both? Why?

b. Assuming a civil action, what problem would the hotel face with regard to *in personam* jurisdiction?

c. Assuming a criminal action, what would the state have to prove in court? What would the hotel recover if prosecution by the state was successful (i.e., the state "won")?

d. Assuming the six fraternity brothers were tried on criminal charges in Florida and acquitted, what lawsuit could they then bring against the Oceanside Luxury Hotel? What standard does the law impose to determine the hotel's liability?

CHAPTER 25

International Aspects of
Innkeeper-Guest Liability

Causes of action recognized in U.S. law for breach of contract (including reservation), personal injury, and loss of property are greatly complicated by the absence of such laws in other jurisdictions as well as by the inconvenience of bringing a lawsuit in a different country. If adopted, the Convention on the Hotelkeeper's Contract drafted by the International Institute for the Unification of Private Law (UNIDROIT) would bring uniformity to these problems and make resolution of them easier for foreign travelers.

CHAPTER 26

Employment Law

I. The employer-employee relationship (24:1).
   A. Many employees are hired "at will," that is, the employer-employee contract does not have a definite term, and therefore the employee may be discharged at any time. *Employee can quit at any time.*
   B. Some at-will employees who have been dismissed have sued their employers.
      1. In *Palmateer v. International Harvester Co.* (textbook, pp. 803–8), an Illinois court held that an employee who "blew the whistle" (reported a crime) and was then fired could sue for the tort of retaliatory discharge because the firing violated public policy (the reporting of crimes).
      2. In a California decision, the court held that they would not allow a lawsuit based on tort theory for the same type of whistle blowing as mentioned above in the Illinois case, but that the fired employee could sue for breach of contract. *Foley v. Interactive Data Corp.* (textbook, pp. 808–10).
II. Employment discrimination (24:2).
   A. Sex discrimination.
      1. Federal law prohibiting sex discrimination is contained in Title VII of the Civil Rights Act of 1964.
      2. State law varies among the states. (See Chapter 4.)
   B. Age discrimination (24:3).

(handwritten top margin) — Employer may not medically examine you to see if you are disabled.

1. Federal law prohibiting age discrimination is contained in the ADEA (Age Discrimination in Employment Act) and protects those aged 40–70. *(handwritten: 1967)*

(handwritten left margin: — punitive damage if menswear is proven.)

2. Basically, the tenets and <u>defenses</u> of Title VII of the Civil Rights Act apply. *(handwritten: — Bonified qualification)*

   C. Disability (24:4). *(handwritten: — Discharged for good reason.)*

(handwritten left margin: Americans w/ Disab. Act)

1. Federal law prohibiting discrimination on the basis of disability is contained in the Americans with Disabilities Act. *(handwritten: 1990)*

(handwritten left margin:
— Are you disabled
— job open
— q valified for job except for handicap
— denied the job based on handic)

2. Covers persons with AIDS (24:5), drug addiction, alcoholism, cancer, and learning disabilities.

3. Makes it illegal to inquire about disability before hiring.

4. Requires the employer, once a disabled person has been hired, to take steps to accommodate that person as set out in *Whitlock v. Donovan* (textbook, pp. 820–25). *(handwritten: Hostile– Sexual harrasment in an environmer)*

III. Sexual harassment (24:6). *(handwritten: Quid Pro Quo– harrasment directed to you person)*

   A. Title VII of the Civil Rights Act of 1964 covers sexual harassment, which includes both exchanges of sex for job favors and the creation of a hostile environment through sexual innuendo (jokes, lewd comments, and so on).

   B. The employer is liable if he or she "knew or should have known" of sexual harassment taking place in the workplace. *Meritor Savings Bank v. Vinson* (textbook, pp. 826–30).

   C. To prevail in a hostile environment, sexual harassment case, the plaintiff must prove that she or he is subject to unwelcome verbal conduct or to displays of a sexual nature that create an "intimidating, hostile, or offensive working environment." *Rabidue v. Osceola Refining Co.* (textbook, pp. 831–34).

   D. In *Broderick v. Ruder* (textbook, pp. 835–39), evidence of constant sexual remarks and gestures, favors granted to women in the office who granted sexual favors to men, and repeated complaints by the plaintiff about the sexual environment were all evidence of sexual harassment in a division office of the SEC.

   E. The employer has liability for sexual harassment by a supervising

(handwritten left margin, vertical:
3 Requirements
↑ all women
↑ Non caucasian
↑ No member of protected class)

(handwritten bottom:
Work discrimination
Disparate – specifically discriminated against
Disparate effect – make conditions intolerable so you can't work. Not directed at the individual, but at a group/class of people)

employee who has broad authority over employment decisions
and who abuses that discretion by harassing another employee.
Craig v. Y and Y Snacks, Inc. (textbook, pp. 839–41).

IV. Alcohol and drug testing (24:7).

    A. Americans with Disabilities Act. *Don't have to hire an Alcoholic or Drug Addict*

        1. Protects addicts who have completed a rehabilitation program
and are no longer engaged in use of illegal drugs, or who are
alcohol-free.

        2. Does not protect "active" drug users or alcoholics.

    B. Testing.

        1. Employers are allowed to use drug testing to ensure that em-
ployees are drug-free, but the testing must be done reasonably
contemporaneous to work, with notice, and only to ensure a
safe work environment. *Luedke v. Nabors Alaska Drilling
Company,* (textbook, pp. 842–43).

V. Employee safety and health (24:8).

    A. The Occupational Safety and Health Act (OSHA) is the federal
law that protects the health and safety of workers.

provide safe env. free from apparent danger regardless of cost.

        1. The Occupational Safety and Health Administration adminis-
ters health and safety standards in the workplace.

        2. The act protects an employee from retaliation for refusing to
perform a task that the employee fears may cause death or
serious injury. *Whirlpool Corp. v. Marshall* (textbook, p.
844).

    B. Workers' compensation (24:9).

worker can get recovery from

        1. Workers' compensation is a set of state laws that compensates
employees or their families for injuries or death on the job.

        2. Most states do not allow recovery for mental suffering, but
Minnesota did allow recovery for a stress-induced ulcer in
Egeland v. City of Minneapolis (textbook, pp. 849–52).

Worker suing third party

Can recover { - Recovery for mental condition causing by physical injury.
{ - Physical injury causing mental injury

Can't recover - mental stress causes mental harm mental condition?

Review Questions for Chapters 3, 4, 26 and Textbook, Chapters 4 and 24

Your answers to the following questions should be based on rules and cases, not on opinion or facts.

1. You are the personnel manager of the Fabulous Hotel, located in New York State. Last year you hired Jerry Grumble as an evening maintenance supervisor. Unfortunately, Jerry is not working out because he has an attitude problem, is chronically late to work, and has not been performing his duties.
   a. Assume that Jerry has no employment contract with the Fabulous. What kind of employee is he classified as, and what steps can you take to fire him?
   b. Assume that Jerry has a contract for a term of one year with your company. What impact will this have on firing him?
   c. Before this problem arises, what personnel procedures should the Fabulous have in place to avoid legal problems?
   d. What additional liability would the hotel have if six months ago, Jerry had reported a major problem with asbestos at the hotel to the Occupational Safety and Health Administration? Discuss.
   e. What additional liability would the hotel have if Jerry was between 40 and 70 years old? Discuss.

CHAPTER 27

Environmental Law and Land Use

I. Common-law environmental claims (25:1).
    A. Nuisance is a tort that interferes with another's right to use his or her land—for example, a smelly pig farm or a discharge of smoke from a factory.
    B. In *California Tahoe Regional Planning Agency v. Jennings* (textbook, pp. 853–56), the court stated that to prevail in a nuisance case and to have the court issue an injunction halting the building of high-rise hotels, the plaintiff must show that the danger is real and immediate.
II. Government regulation of toxic and hazardous substances (25:2).
    A. Federal laws that protect the environment include the Clean Water Act and the Toxic Substances Control Act.
    B. The government may impose penalties for violations of regulations pertaining to toxic substances such as asbestos in buildings. *U.S. v. Tzavah Urban Renewal Corp.* (textbook, pp. 857–59).
III. Private enforcement (25:3).
    A. Private citizens may bring environmental lawsuits (have standing to sue) if they can show that injury occurred and that the injury was sustained within the zone the government was trying to protect.
    B. For a private person to bring an action, he must show that he himself is injured. In *Sierra Club v. Morton* (textbook, p. 859),

[187]

the Sierra Club failed to allege that it or its members would be affected in any of their activities or pasttimes by the Disney development.

IV. Liability of private parties (25:5).

    A. A private developer must file an Environmental Impact Statement (EIS) before construction begins. *Citizens of Croleta Valley v. Board of Supervisors* (textbook, p. 875).

    B. The environment, for purposes of the EIS, includes population concentration, distribution, or growth, and the character of the neighborhood. *Chinese Staff and Workers Association v. City of New York* (textbook, pp. 864–66).

V. Regulation of land use (25:6).

    A. Environmental cases.

        1. In *League to Save Lake Tahoe v. Trounday*, 427 F. Supp. 1350 (D. Nev. 1977), *affirmed* 598 F.2d 1164 (9th Cir. 1979), *cert. denied* 444 U.S. 943, 62 L. Ed. 2d 310 (1979), the court held that a federal court review of an administrative decision entrusted by Congress to state officials is not proper.

        2. In *People of Saipan v. United States Department of the Interior*, 356 F. Supp. 645 (D. Hawaii 1973), the court stated that actions by the top government official who signed a lease allowing construction of a hotel were not the actions of a federal agency and therefore were not reviewable by the EPA or under the Environmental Protection Act.

        3. The California Coastal Commission has the authority to stop the construction of a hotel when there is substantial evidence of risk to the marsh environment. *City of Chula Vista v. Superior Court of San Diego County* (textbook, p. 867).

        4. In *City of Carmel by the Sea v. Board of Supervisors of Monterey County*, 137 Cal. App. 3d 964, 187, Cal. Rptr. 379 (1983), the failure of a local planning board to comply with State Office of Planning and Research conditions invalidated a building permit.

5. In *Conservation Law Foundation of New England, Inc. v. Secretary of the Interior* (textbook, pp. 875–76), adequate ecological protection was determined on the basis of data and methodology showing that there was no erosion to coastal areas caused by the use of off-road vehicles.

B. For a review of materials pertaining to the federal Endangered Species Act, the Wilderness Act, the National Historic Preservation Act, and Land Use Permits, see *Wilson v. Block* (textbook, pp. 868–73). For a review of federal environmental laws in general, see *Vieux Carre Property v. Pierce*, 719 F.2d 1272 (5th Cir. 1983).

C. Exhaustion of administrative remedies. Before going to court, plaintiffs must go through administrative channels. *Coalition for Student Action v. City of Fullerton* (textbook, pp. 873–74).

Review Questions for Chapter 27 and Textbook, Chapter 25

Your answers to the following questions should be based on rules and cases, not on opinion or facts.

1. Distinguish between a common law environmental claim and a statutory claim. What are the underlying legal theories upon which a plaintiff could bring each type of claim?

2. The Andersons purchased a home in a rural section of New York State. Upon moving into the new home, they noticed a pervasive odor in the neighborhood which, after investigation, turned out to be a pig farm. The pig farm was established in 1956. The Andersons purchased their home in 1992. Will the Andersons prevail in a lawsuit based on nuisance? Suppose the situation was reversed and the Andersons arrived before the pig farm? Would this make any difference?

3. What is meant by the phrase "standing to sue"? Please give an

example in which a person would not have standing to sue in an environmental lawsuit against a fictitious polluter located in the United States.

4. What is meant by the phrase "exhaustion of administrative remedies"? What impact does this requirement have upon environmental litigation?

5. Briefly compare and contrast the Endangered Species Act, Wilderness Act, and National Historic Preservation Act.

CHAPTER 28

Catastrophic Risk Liability

I. Insurance (26:1).
   A. The purpose of insurance is to provide for those situations in which an unpredictable event may result in money liability.
II. Contract theory (26:2). Impossibility of providing substitute performance discharges parties.
III. Tort theory (26:3).
   A. Acts of God may discharge parties (26:4).
   B. Waivers of liability signed by guests may protect the innkeeper in some states.
   C. The innkeeper may have a duty to provide reasonable rescue, first aid, and other assistance in case of terrorist activity (26:6).
IV. Property (26:4). Acts of God and acts of a Public Enemy may excuse the innkeeper from liability for property.

Review Questions for Chapter 28 and Textbook, Chapter 26

Your answers to the following questions should be based on rules and cases, not on opinion or facts.

1. What are the major purposes of obtaining insurance? What are some of the factors you would consider as a manager in determining whether to insure and the appropriate amount of coverage?

2. The Fabulous Hotel is located on a landfill at the mouth of the Mississippi River in New Orleans. What is the difference in the type of insurance coverage appropriate in the event the hotel is destroyed by a flood? A hurricane? Eroding land from natural causes? A fire set by an employee?

3. The American-owned Fancy Hotel is located in a country at war with the United States. The Fancy routinely provides accommodations to American tourists. Assuming that a terrorist takeover of the Fancy Hotel results in injuries to American guests at the hotel, what liability does the hotel have? Can the hotel successfully argue any defenses?

APPENDIX

The United States Constitution

We the People of the United States, in Order to form a more perfect Union, establish Justice, insure domestic Tranquility, provide for the common defence, promote the general Welfare, and secure the Blessings of Liberty to ourselves and our Posterity, do ordain and establish this Constitution for the United States of America.

ARTICLE I

Section 1.   All legislative Powers herein granted shall be vested in a Congress of the United States, which shall consist of a Senate and House of Representatives.

Section 2.   The House of Representatives shall be composed of Members chosen every second Year by the People of the several States, and the Electors in each State shall have the Qualifications requisite for Electors of the most numerous Branch of the State Legislature.

No Person shall be a Representative who shall not have attained to the Age of twenty five Years, and been seven Years a Citizen of the United States, and who shall not, when elected, be an Inhabitant of that State in which he shall be chosen.

Representatives and direct Taxes shall be apportioned among the several States which may be included within this Union, according to their respective Numbers, which shall be determined by adding to the whole Number of free Persons, including those bound to Service for a Term of Years, and excluding Indians not taxed, three fifths of all other Persons. The actual Enumeration shall be made within three Years after the first Meeting of the Congress of the United States, and within every subsequent Term of ten Years, in such Manner as they shall by Law direct. The Number of Representatives shall not exceed one for every thirty Thousand, but each State shall have at Least one Representative; and until such enumeration shall be made, the State of New Hampshire shall be entitled to chuse three, Massachusetts eight, Rhode Island and Providence Plantations one, Connecticut five, New York six, New Jersey four, Pennsylvania eight, Delaware one, Maryland six, Virginia ten, North Carolina five, South Carolina five, and Georgia three.

When vacancies happen in the Representation from any State, the Executive Authority thereof shall issue Writs of Election to fill such Vacancies.

The House of Representatives shall chuse their Speaker and other Officers; and shall have the sole Power of Impeachment.

Section 3.   The Senate of the United States shall be composed of two Senators from each State, chosen by the Legislature thereof, for six Years; and each Senator shall have one Vote.

Immediately after they shall be assembled in Consequence of the first Election, they shall be divided as equally as may be into three Classes. The Seats of the Senators of the first Class shall be vacated at the Expiration of the second Year, of the second Class at the Expiration of the fourth Year, and of the third Class at the Expiration of the sixth Year, so that one third may be chosen every second Year; and if Vacancies happen by Resignation, or otherwise, during the Recess of the Legislature of any State, the Executive thereof may make temporary Appointments until the next Meeting of the Legislature, which shall then fill such Vacancies.

No Person shall be a Senator who shall not have attained to the Age of thirty Years, and been nine Years a Citizen of the United States, and who shall not, when elected, be an Inhabitant of that State for which he shall be chosen.

The Vice President of the United States shall be President of the Senate, but shall have no Vote, unless they be equally divided.

The Senate shall chuse their other Officers, and also a President pro tempore, in the Absence of the Vice President, or when he shall exercise the Office of President of the United States.

The Senate shall have the sole Power to try all Impeachments. When sitting for that Purpose, they shall be on Oath or Affirmation. When the President of the United States is tried, the Chief Justice shall preside: And no Person shall be convicted without the Concurrence of two thirds of the Members present.

Judgment in Cases of Impeachment shall not extend further than to removal from Office, and disqualification to hold and enjoy any Office of honor, Trust, or Profit under the United States: but the Party convicted shall nevertheless be liable and subject to Indictment, Trial, Judgment, and Punishment, according to Law.

Section 4.   The Times, Places and Manner of holding Elections for Senators and Representatives, shall be prescribed in each State by the Legislature thereof; but the Congress may at any time by Law make or alter such Regulations, except as to the Places of chusing Senators.

The Congress shall assemble at least once in every Year, and such Meeting shall be on the first Monday in December, unless they shall by Law appoint a different Day.

Section 5.   Each House shall be the Judge of the Elections, Returns, and Qualifications of its own Members, and a Majority of each shall constitute a Quorum to do Business; but a smaller Number may adjourn from day to day, and may be authorized to compel the Attendance of absent Members, in such Manner, and under such Penalties as each House may provide.

Each House may determine the Rules of its Proceedings, punish its Members for disorderly Behavior, and, with the Concurrence of two thirds, expel a Member.

Each House shall keep a Journal of its Proceedings, and from time to time publish the same, excepting such Parts as may in their Judgment require Secrecy; and the Yeas and Nays of the Members of either House on any question shall, at the Desire of one fifth of those Present, be entered on the Journal.

Neither House, during the Session of Congress, shall, without the Consent of the other, adjourn for more than three days, nor to any other Place than that in which the two Houses shall be sitting.

Section 6.   The Senators and Representatives shall receive a Compensation for their Services, to be ascertained by Law, and paid out of the Treasury of the United States. They shall in all Cases, except Treason, Felony and Breach of the Peace, be privileged from Arrest during their Attendance at the Session of their respective Houses, and in going to and returning from the same; and for any Speech or Debate in either House, they shall not be questioned in any other Place.

No Senator or Representative shall, during the Time for which he was elected, be appointed to any civil Office under the Authority of the United States, which shall have been created, or the Emoluments whereof shall have been increased during such time; and no Person holding any Office under the United States, shall be a Member of either House during his Continuance in Office.

Section 7.   All Bills for raising Revenue shall originate in the House of Representatives; but the Senate may propose or concur with Amendments as on other Bills.

Every Bill which shall have passed the House of Representatives and the Senate, shall, before it become a Law, be presented to the President of the United States; If he approve he shall sign it, but if not he shall return it, with his Objections to the House in which it shall have originated, who shall enter the Objections at large on their Journal, and proceed to reconsider it. If after such Reconsideration two thirds of that House shall agree to pass the Bill, it shall be sent together with the Objections, to the other House, by which it shall likewise be reconsidered, and if approved by two thirds of that House, it shall become a Law. But in all such Cases the Votes of both Houses shall be determined by Yeas and Nays, and the Names of the Persons voting for and against the Bill shall be entered on the Journal of each House respectively. If any Bill shall not be returned by the President within ten Days (Sundays excepted) after it shall have been presented to him, the Same shall be a Law, in like Manner as if he had signed it, unless the Congress by their Adjournment prevent its Return in which Case it shall not be a Law.

Every Order, Resolution, or Vote, to which the Concurrence of the Senate and House of Representatives may be necessary (except on a question of Adjournment) shall be presented to the President of the United States; and before the Same shall take Effect, shall be approved by him, or being disapproved by him, shall be repassed by two thirds of the Senate and House of Representatives, according to the Rules and Limitations prescribed in the Case of a Bill.

Section 8.   The Congress shall have Power To lay and collect Taxes, Duties, Imposts and Excises, to pay the Debts and provide for the common Defence and general Welfare of the United States; but all Duties, Imposts and Excises shall be uniform throughout the United States;

To borrow Money on the credit of the United States;

To regulate Commerce with foreign Nations, and among the several States, and with the Indian Tribes;

To establish an uniform Rule of Naturalization, and uniform Laws on the subject of Bankruptcies throughout the United States;

To coin Money, regulate the Value thereof, and of foreign Coin, and fix the Standard of Weights and Measures;

To provide for the Punishment of counterfeiting the Securities and current Coin of the United States;

To establish Post Offices and post Roads;

To promote the Progress of Science and useful Arts, by securing for limited Times to Authors and Inventors the exclusive Right to their respective Writings and Discoveries;

To constitute Tribunals inferior to the supreme Court;

To define and punish Piracies and Felonies committed on the high Seas, and Offenses against the Law of Nations;

To declare War, grant Letters of Marque and Reprisal, and make Rules concerning Captures on Land and Water;

To raise and support Armies, but no Appropriation of Money to that Use shall be for a longer Term than two Years;

To provide and maintain a Navy;

To make Rules for the Government and Regulation of the land and naval Forces;

To provide for calling forth the Militia to execute the Laws of the Union, suppress Insurrections and repel Invasions;

To provide for organizing, arming, and disciplining, the Militia, and for governing such Part of them as may be employed in the Service of the United States, reserving to the States respectively, the Appointment of the Officers, and the Authority of training the Militia according to the discipline prescribed by Congress;

To exercise exclusive Legislation in all Cases whatsoever, over such District (not exceeding ten Miles square) as may, by Cession of particular States, and the Acceptance of Congress, become the Seat of the Government of the United States, and to exercise like Authority over all Places purchased by the Consent of the Legislature of the State in which the Same shall be, for the Erection of Forts, Magazines, Arsenals, dock-Yards, and other needful Buildings;—And

To make all Laws which shall be necessary and proper for carrying into Execution the foregoing Powers, and all other Powers vested by this Constitution in the Government of the United States, or in any Department or Officer thereof.

Section 9.   The Migration or Importation of such Persons as any of the States now existing shall think proper to admit, shall not be prohibited by the Congress prior to the Year one thousand eight hundred and eight, but a Tax or duty may be imposed on such Importation, not exceeding ten dollars for each Person.

The privilege of the Writ of Habeas Corpus shall not be suspended, unless when in Cases of Rebellion or Invasion the public Safety may require it.

No Bill of Attainder or ex post facto Law shall be passed.

No Capitation, or other direct, Tax shall be laid, unless in Proportion to the Census or Enumeration herein before directed to be taken.

No Tax or Duty shall be laid on Articles exported from any State.

No Preference shall be given by any Regulation of Commerce or Revenue to the Ports of one State over those of another: nor shall Vessels bound to, or from, one State be obliged to enter, clear, or pay Duties in another.

No Money shall be drawn from the Treasury, but in Consequence of Appropriations made by Law; and a regular Statement and Account of the Receipts and Expenditures of all public Money shall be published from time to time.

No Title of Nobility shall be granted by the United States: And no Person holding any Office of Profit or Trust under them, shall, without the Consent of the Congress, accept of any present, Emolument, Office, or Title, of any kind whatever, from any King, Prince, or foreign State.

Section 10.   No State shall enter into any Treaty, Alliance, or Confederation; grant Letters of Marque and Reprisal; coin Money; emit Bills of Credit; make any Thing but gold and silver Coin a Tender in Payment of Debts; pass any Bill of

Attainder, ex post facto Law, or Law impairing the Obligation of Contracts, or grant any Title of Nobility.

No State shall, without the Consent of the Congress, lay any Imposts or Duties on Imports or Exports, except what may be absolutely necessary for executing its inspection Laws: and the net Produce of all Duties and Imposts, laid by any State on Imports or Exports, shall be for the Use of the Treasury of the United States; and all such Laws shall be subject to the Revision and Control of the Congress.

No State shall, without the Consent of Congress, lay any Duty of Tonnage, keep Troops, or Ships of War in time of Peace, enter into any Agreement or Compact with another State, or with a foreign Power, or engage in War, unless actually invaded, or in such imminent Danger as will not admit of delay.

ARTICLE II

Section 1.   The executive Power shall be vested in a President of the United States of America. He shall hold his Office during the Term of four Years, and, together with the Vice President, chosen for the same Term, be elected, as follows:

Each State shall appoint, in such Manner as the Legislature thereof may direct, a Number of Electors, equal to the whole Number of Senators and Representatives to which the State may be entitled in the Congress; but no Senator or Representative, or Person holding an Office of Trust or Profit under the United States, shall be appointed an Elector.

The Electors shall meet in their respective States, and vote by Ballot for two Persons, of whom one at least shall not be an Inhabitant of the same State with themselves. And they shall make a List of all the Persons voted for, and of the Number of Votes for each; which List they shall sign and certify, and transmit sealed to the Seat of the Government of the United States, directed to the President of the Senate. The President of the Senate shall, in the Presence of the Senate and House of Representatives, open all the Certificates, and the Votes shall then be counted. The Person having the greatest Number of Votes shall be the President, if such Number be a Majority of the whole Number of Electors appointed; and if there be more than one who have such Majority, and have an equal Number of Votes, then the House of Representatives shall immediately chuse by Ballot one of them for President; and if no Person have a Majority, then from the five highest on the List the said House shall in like Manner chuse the President. But in chusing the President, the Votes shall be taken by States, the Representation from each State having one Vote; A quorum for this Purpose shall consist of a Member or Members from two thirds of the States, and a Majority of all the States shall be necessary to a Choice. In every Case, after the Choice of the President, the Person having the greater Number of Votes of the Electors shall be the Vice President. But if there should remain two or more who have equal Votes, the Senate shall chuse from them by Ballot the Vice President.

The Congress may determine the Time of chusing the Electors, and the Day on which they shall give their Votes; which Day shall be the same throughout the United States.

No person except a natural born Citizen, or a Citizen of the United States, at the time of the Adoption of this Constitution, shall be eligible to the Office of President; neither shall any Person be eligible to that Office who shall not have attained to the Age of thirty five Years, and been fourteen Years a Resident within the United States.

In Case of the Removal of the President from Office, or of his Death, Resignation or Inability to discharge the Powers and Duties of the said Office, the same shall devolve on the Vice President, and the Congress may by Law provide for the Case of Removal, Death, Resignation or Inability, both of the President and Vice President, declaring what Officer shall then act as President, and such Officer shall act accordingly, until the Disability be removed, or a President shall be elected.

The President shall, at stated Times, receive for his Services, a Compensation, which shall neither be increased nor diminished during the Period for which he shall have been elected, and he shall not receive within that Period any other Emolument from the United States, or any of them.

Before he enter on the Execution of his Office, he shall take the following Oath or Affirmation: "I do solemnly swear (or affirm) that I will faithfully execute the Office of President of the United States, and will to the best of my Ability, preserve, protect and defend the Constitution of the United States."

Section 2.   The President shall be Commander in Chief of the Army and Navy of the United States, and of the Militia of the several States, when called into the actual Service of the United States; he may require the Opinion, in writing, of the principal Officer in each of the executive Departments, upon any Subject relating to the Duties of their respective Offices, and he shall have Power to grant Reprieves and Pardons for Offenses against the United States, except in Cases of Impeachment.

He shall have Power, by and with the Advice and Consent of the Senate to make Treaties, provided two thirds of the Senators present concur; and he shall nominate, and by and with the Advice and Consent of the Senate, shall appoint Ambassadors, other public Ministers and Consuls, Judges of the supreme Court, and all other Officers of the United States, whose Appointments are not herein otherwise provided for, and which shall be established by Law; but the Congress may by Law vest the Appointment of such inferior Officers, as they think proper, in the President alone, in the Courts of Law, or in the Heads of Departments.

The President shall have Power to fill up all Vacancies that may happen during the Recess of the Senate, by granting Commissions which shall expire at the End of their next Session.

Section 3.   He shall from time to time give to the Congress Information of the State of the Union, and recommend to their Consideration such Measures as he shall judge necessary and expedient; he may, on extraordinary Occasions, convene both Houses, or either of them, and in Case of Disagreement between them, with Respect to the Time of Adjournment, he may adjourn them to such Time as he shall think proper; he shall receive Ambassadors and other public Ministers; he shall take Care that the Laws be faithfully executed, and shall Commission all the Officers of the United States.

Section 4.   The President, Vice President and all civil Officers of the United States, shall be removed from Office on Impeachment for, and Conviction of, Treason, Bribery, or other high Crimes and Misdemeanors.

ARTICLE III

Section 1.   The judicial Power of the United States, shall be vested in one supreme Court, and in such inferior Courts as the Congress may from time to time ordain and establish. The Judges, both of the supreme and inferior Courts, shall hold their Offices during good Behaviour, and shall, at stated Times, receive for their Services a Compensation, which shall not be diminished during their Continuance in Office.

Section 2.   The judicial Power shall extend to all Cases, in Law and Equity, arising under this Constitution, the Laws of the United States, and Treaties made, or which shall be made, under their Authority;—to all Cases affecting Ambassadors, other public Ministers and Consuls;—to all Cases of admiralty and maritime Jurisdiction;—to Controversies to which the United States shall be a Party;—to Controversies between two or more States;—between a State and Citizens of another State;—between Citizens of different States;—between Citizens of the same State claiming Lands under Grants of different States, and between a State, or the Citizens thereof, and foreign States, Citizens or Subjects.

In all Cases affecting Ambassadors, other public Ministers and Consuls, and those in which a State shall be a Party, the supreme Court shall have original Jurisdiction. In all the other Cases before mentioned, the supreme Court shall have appellate Jurisdiction, both as to Law and Fact, with such Exceptions, and under such Regulations as the Congress shall make.

The Trial of all Crimes, except in Cases of Impeachment, shall be by Jury; and such Trial shall be held in the State where the said Crimes shall have been committed; but when not committed within any State, the Trial shall be at such Place or Places as the Congress may by Law have directed.

Section 3. Treason against the United States, shall consist only in levying War against them, or, in adhering to their Enemies, giving them Aid and Comfort. No Person shall be convicted of Treason unless on the Testimony of two Witnesses to the same overt Act, or on Confession in open Court.

The Congress shall have Power to declare the Punishment of Treason, but no Attainder of Treason shall work Corruption of Blood, or Forfeiture except during the Life of the Person attainted.

ARTICLE IV

Section 1. Full Faith and Credit shall be given in each State to the public Acts, Records, and judicial Proceedings of every other State. And the Congress may by general Laws prescribe the Manner in which such Acts, Records and Proceedings shall be proved, and the Effect thereof.

Section 2. The Citizens of each State shall be entitled to all Privileges and Immunities of Citizens in the several States.

A Person charged in any State with Treason, Felony, or other Crime, who shall flee from Justice, and be found in another State, shall on Demand of the executive Authority of the State from which he fled, be delivered up, to be removed to the State having Jurisdiction of the Crime.

No Person held to Service or Labour in one State, under the Laws thereof, escaping into another, shall, in Consequence of any Law or Regulation therein, be discharged from such Service or Labour, but shall be delivered up on Claim of the Party to whom such Service or Labour may be due.

Section 3. New States may be admitted by the Congress into this Union; but no new State shall be formed or erected within the Jurisdiction of any other State; nor any State be formed by the Junction of two or more States, or Parts of States, without the Consent of the Legislatures of the States concerned as well as of the Congress.

The Congress shall have Power to dispose of and make all needful Rules and Regulations respecting the Territory or other Property belonging to the United States; and nothing in this Constitution shall be so construed as to Prejudice any Claims of the United States, or of any particular State.

Section 4.   The United States shall guarantee to every State in this Union a Republican Form of Government, and shall protect each of them against Invasion; and on Application of the Legislature, or of the Executive (when the Legislature cannot be convened) against domestic Violence.

ARTICLE V

The Congress, whenever two thirds of both Houses shall deem it necessary, shall propose Amendments to this Constitution, or, on the Application of the Legislatures of two thirds of the several States, shall call a Convention for proposing Amendments, which, in either Case, shall be valid to all Intents and Purposes, as part of this Constitution, when ratified by the Legislatures of three fourths of the several States, or by Conventions in three fourths thereof, as the one or the other Mode of Ratification may be proposed by the Congress; Provided that no Amendment which may be made prior to the Year One thousand eight hundred and eight shall in any Manner affect the first and fourth Clauses in the Ninth Section of the first Article; and that no State, without its Consent, shall be deprived of its equal Suffrage in the Senate.

ARTICLE VI

All Debts contracted and Engagements entered into, before the Adoption of this Constitution shall be as valid against the United States under this Constitution, as under the Confederation.

This Constitution, and the Laws of the United States which shall be made in Pursuance thereof; and all Treaties made, or which shall be made, under the Authority of the United States, shall be the supreme Law of the Land; and the Judges in every State shall be bound thereby, any Thing in the Constitution or Laws of any State to the Contrary notwithstanding.

The Senators and Representatives before mentioned, and the Members of the several State Legislatures, and all executive and judicial Officers, both of the United States and of the several States, shall be bound by Oath or Affirmation, to support this Constitution; but no religious Test shall ever be required as a Qualification to any Office or public Trust under the United States.

ARTICLE VII

The Ratification of the Conventions of nine States shall be sufficient for the Establishment of this Constitution between the States so ratifying the Same.

AMENDMENT I [1791]

Congress shall make no law respecting an establishment of religion, or prohibiting the free exercise thereof; or abridging the freedom of speech, or of the press; or the right of the people peaceably to assemble, and to petition the Government for a redress of grievances.

AMENDMENT II [1791]

A well regulated Militia, being necessary to the security of a free State, the right of the people to keep and bear Arms, shall not be infringed.

AMENDMENT III [1791]

No Soldier shall, in time of peace be quartered in any house, without the consent of the Owner, nor in time of war, but in a manner to be prescribed by law.

AMENDMENT IV [1791]

The right of the people to be secure in their persons, houses, papers, and effects, against unreasonable searches and seizures, shall not be violated, and no Warrants shall issue, but upon probable cause, supported by Oath or affirmation, and particularly describing the place to be searched, and the persons or things to be seized.

AMENDMENT V [1791]

No person shall be held to answer for a capital, or otherwise infamous crime, unless on a presentment or indictment of a Grand Jury, except in cases arising in the land or naval forces, or in the Militia, when in actual service in time of War or public danger; nor shall any person be subject for the same offence to be twice put in jeopardy of life or limb; nor shall be compelled in any criminal case to be a witness against himself, nor be deprived of life, liberty, or property, without due process of law; nor shall private property be taken for public use, without just compensation.

AMENDMENT VI [1791]

In all criminal prosecutions, the accused shall enjoy the right to a speedy and public trial, by an impartial jury of the State and district wherein the crime shall have been committed, which district shall have been previously ascertained by law, and to be informed of the nature and cause of the accusation; to be confronted with the witnesses against him; to have compulsory process for obtaining witness in his favor, and to have the Assistance of Counsel for his defence.

AMENDMENT VII [1791]

In Suits at common law, where the value in controversy shall exceed twenty dollars, the right of trial by jury shall be preserved, and no fact tried by jury, shall be otherwise re-examined in any Court of the United States, than according to the rules of the common law.

AMENDMENT VIII [1791]

Excessive bail shall not be required, nor excessive fines imposed, nor cruel and unusual punishments inflicted.

AMENDMENT IX [1791]

The enumeration in the Constitution, of certain rights, shall not be construed to deny or disparage others retained by the people.

AMENDMENT X [1791]

The powers not delegated to the United States by the Constitution, nor prohibited by it to the States, are reserved to the States respectively, or to the people.

AMENDMENT XI [1798]

The Judicial power of the United States shall not be construed to extend to any suit in law or equity, commenced or prosecuted against one of the United States by Citizens of another State, or by Citizens or Subjects of any Foreign State.

AMENDMENT XII [1804]

The Electors shall meet in their respective states, and vote by ballot for President and Vice-President, one of whom, at least, shall not be an inhabitant of the same state with themselves; they shall name in their ballots the person voted for as President, and in distinct ballots the person voted for as Vice-President, and they shall make distinct lists of all persons voted for as President, and of all persons voted for as Vice-President, and of the number of votes for each, which lists they shall sign and certify, and transmit sealed to the seat of the government of the United States, directed to the President of the Senate;—The President of the Senate shall, in the presence of the Senate and House of Representatives, open all the certificates and the votes shall then be counted;—The person having the greatest number of votes for President, shall be the President, if such number be a majority of the whole number of Electors appointed; and if no person have such majority, then from the persons having the highest numbers not exceeding three on the list of those voted for as President, the House of Representatives shall choose immediately, by ballot, the President. But in choosing the President, the votes shall be taken by states, the representation from each state having one vote; a quorum for this purpose shall consist of a member or members from two-thirds of the states, and a majority of all states shall be necessary to a choice. And if the House of Representatives shall not choose a President whenever the right of choice shall devolve upon them, before the fourth day of March next following, then the Vice-President shall act as President, as in the case of the death or other constitutional disability of the President.—The person having the greatest number of votes as Vice-President, shall be the Vice-President, if such number be a majority of the whole number of Electors appointed, and if no person have a majority, then from the two highest numbers on the list, the Senate shall choose the Vice-President; a quorum for the purpose shall consist of two-thirds of the whole number of Senators, and a majority of the whole number shall be necessary to a choice. But no person constitutionally ineligible to the office of President shall be eligible to that of Vice-President of the United States.

AMENDMENT XIII [1865]

Section 1.   Neither slavery nor involuntary servitude, except as a punishment for crime whereof the party shall have been duly convicted, shall exist within the United States, or any place subject to their jurisdiction.

Section 2.   Congress shall have power to enforce this article by appropriate legislation.

AMENDMENT XIV [1868]

Section 1.   All persons born or naturalized in the United States, and subject to the jurisdiction thereof, are citizens of the United States and of the State wherein they reside. No State shall make or enforce any law which shall abridge the privileges or immunities of citizens of the United States; nor shall any State deprive any person of life, liberty, or property, without due process of law; nor deny to any person within its jurisdiction the equal protection of the laws.

Section 2.   Representatives shall be apportioned among the several States according to their respective numbers, counting the whole number of persons in each State, excluding Indians not taxed. But when the right to vote at any election for the choice of electors for President and Vice President of the United States, Representatives in Congress, the Executive and Judicial officers of a State, or the members of the Legislature thereof, is denied to any of the male inhabitants of such State, being twenty-one years of age, and citizens of the United States, or in any way abridged, except for participation in rebellion, or other crime, the basis of representation therein shall be reduced in the proportion which the number of such male citizens shall bear to the whole number of male citizens twenty-one years of age in such State.

Section 3.   No person shall be a Senator or Representative in Congress, or elector of President and Vice President, or hold any office, civil or military, under the United States, or under any State, who having previously taken an oath, as a member of Congress, or as an officer of the United States, or as a member of any State legislature, or as an executive or judicial officer of any State, to support the Constitution of the United States, shall have engaged in insurrection or rebellion against the same, or given aid or comfort to the enemies thereof. But Congress may by a vote of two-thirds of each House, remove such disability.

Section 4.   The validity of the public debt of the United States, authorized by law, including debts incurred for payment of pensions and bounties for services in suppressing insurrection or rebellion, shall not be questioned. But neither the United States nor any State shall assume or pay any debt or obligation incurred in aid of insurrection or rebellion against the United States, or any claim for the loss or emancipation of any slave; but all such debts, obligations and claims shall be held illegal and void.

Section 5.   The Congress shall have power to enforce, by appropriate legislation, the provisions of this article.

AMENDMENT XV [1870]

Section 1.   The right of citizens of the United States to vote shall not be denied or abridged by the United States or by any State on account of race, color, or previous condition of servitude.

Section 2.   The Congress shall have power to enforce this article by appropriate legislation.

AMENDMENT XVI [1913]

The Congress shall have power to lay and collect taxes on incomes, from whatever source derived, without apportionment among the several States, and without regard to any census or enumeration.

AMENDMENT XVII [1913]

The Senate of the United States shall be composed of two Senators from each State, elected by the people thereof, for six years; and each Senator shall have one vote. The electors in each State shall have the qualifications requisite for electors of the most numerous branch of the State legislatures.

When vacancies happen in the representation of any State in the Senate, the executive authority of such State shall issue writs of election to fill such vacancies: *Provided*, That the legislature of any State may empower the executive thereof to make temporary appointments until the people fill the vacancies by election as the legislature may direct.

This amendment shall not be so construed as to affect the election or term of any Senator chosen before it becomes valid as part of the Constitution.

AMENDMENT XVIII [1919]

Section 1.   After one year from the ratification of this article the manufacture, sale, or transportation of intoxicating liquors within, the importation thereof into, or the exportation thereof from the United States and all territory subject to the jurisdiction thereof for beverage purposes is hereby prohibited.

Section 2.   The Congress and the several States shall have concurrent power to enforce this article by appropriate legislation.

Section 3.   This article shall be inoperative unless it shall have been ratified as an amendment to the Constitution by the legislatures of the several States, as provided in the Constitution, within seven years from the date of the submission hereof to the States by the Congress.

AMENDMENT XIX [1920]

The right of citizens of the United States to vote shall not be denied or abridged by the United States or by any State on account of sex.

Congress shall have power to enforce this article by appropriate legislation.

AMENDMENT XX [1933]

Section 1.   The terms of the President and Vice President shall end at noon on the 20th day of January, and the terms of Senators and Representatives at noon on the 3d day of January, of the years in which such terms would have ended if this article had not been ratified; and the terms of their successors shall then begin.

Section 2.   The Congress shall assemble at least once in every year, and such meeting shall begin at noon on the 3d day of January, unless they shall by law appoint a different day.

Section 3.   If, at the time fixed for the beginning of the term of the President, the President elect shall have died, the Vice President elect shall become President. If the President shall not have been chosen before the time fixed for the beginning of his term, or if the President elect shall have failed to qualify, then the Vice President elect shall act as President until a President shall have qualified; and the Congress may by law provide for the case wherein neither a President elect nor a Vice President elect shall have qualified, declaring who shall then act as President, or the manner in which one who is to act shall be selected, and such person shall act accordingly until a President or Vice President shall have qualified.

Section 4.   The Congress may by law provide for the case of the death of any of the persons from whom the House of Representatives may choose a President whenever the right of choice shall have devolved upon them, and for the case of the death of any of the persons from whom the Senate may choose a Vice President whenever the right of choice shall have devolved upon them.

Section 5.   Sections 1 and 2 shall take effect on the 15th day of October following the ratification of this article.

Section 6.   This article shall be inoperative unless it shall have been ratified as an amendment to the Constitution by the legislatures of three-fourths of the several States within seven years from the date of its submission.

AMENDMENT XXI [1933]

Section 1.   The eighteenth article of amendment to the Constitution of the United States is hereby repealed.

Section 2.   The transportation or importation into any State, Territory, or possession of the United States for delivery or use therein of intoxicating liquors, in violation of the laws thereof, is hereby prohibited.

Section 3.   This article shall be inoperative unless it shall have been ratified as an amendment to the Constitution by conventions in the several States, as provided in the Constitution, within seven years from the date of the submission hereof to the States by the Congress.

AMENDMENT XXII [1951]

Section 1.   No person shall be elected to the office of the President more than twice, and no person who has held the office of President, or acted as President, for more than two years of a term to which some other person was elected President shall be elected to the office of President more than once. But this Article shall not apply to any person holding the office of President when this Article was proposed by the Congress, and shall not prevent any person who may be holding the office of President, or acting as President, during the term within which this Article becomes operative from holding the office of President or acting as President during the remainder of such term.

Section 2.   This article shall be inoperative unless it shall have been ratified as an amendment to the Constitution by the legislatures of three-fourths of the several States within seven years from the date of its submission to the States by the Congress.

AMENDMENT XXIII [1961]

Section 1.   The District constituting the seat of Government of the United States shall appoint in such manner as the Congress may direct:

A number of electors of President and Vice President equal to the whole number of Senators and Representatives in Congress to which the District would be entitled if it were a State, but in no event more than the least populous state; they shall be in addition to those appointed by the states, but they shall be considered, for the purposes of the election of President and Vice President, to be electors appointed by a state; and they shall meet in the District and perform such duties as provided by the twelfth article of amendment.

Section 2.   The Congress shall have power to enforce this article by appropriate legislation.

AMENDMENT XXIV [1964]

Section 1.   The right of citizens of the United States to vote in any primary or other election for President or Vice President, for electors for President or Vice President, or for Senator or Representative in Congress, shall not be denied or abridged by the United States, or any State by reason of failure to pay any poll tax or other tax.

Section 2.   The Congress shall have power to enforce this article by appropriate legislation.

AMENDMENT XXV [1967]

Section 1.   In case of the removal of the President from office or of his death or resignation, the Vice President shall become President.

Section 2.   Whenever there is a vacancy in the office of the Vice President, the President shall nominate a Vice President who shall take office upon confirmation by a majority vote of both Houses of Congress.

Section 3.   Whenever the President transmits to the President pro tempore of the Senate and the Speaker of the House of Representatives his written declaration that he is unable to discharge the powers and duties of his office, and until he transmits to them a written declaration to the contrary, such powers and duties shall be discharged by the Vice President as Acting President.

Section 4.   Whenever the Vice President and a majority of either the principal officers of the executive departments or of such other body as Congress may by law provide, transmit to the President pro tempore of the Senate and the Speaker of the House of Representatives their written declaration that the President is unable to discharge the powers and duties of his office, the Vice President shall immediately assume the powers and duties of the office as Acting President.

Thereafter, when the President transmits to the President pro tempore of the Senate and the Speaker of the House of Representatives his written declaration that no inability exists, he shall resume the powers and duties of his office unless the Vice President and a majority of either the principal officers of the executive department or of such other body as Congress may by law provide, transmit within four days to the President pro tempore of the Senate and the Speaker of the House of Representatives their written declaration that the President is unable to discharge the powers and duties of his office. Thereupon Congress shall decide the issue, assembling within forty-eight hours for that purpose if not in session. If the Congress, within twenty-one days after receipt of the latter written declaration, or, if Congress is not in session, within twenty-one days after Congress is required to assemble, determines by two-thirds vote of both Houses that the President is unable to discharge the powers and duties of his office, the Vice President shall continue to discharge the same as Acting President; otherwise, the President shall resume the powers and duties of his office.

AMENDMENT XXVI [1971]

Section 1.   The right of citizens of the United States, who are eighteen years of age or older, to vote shall not be denied or abridged by the United States or by any State on account of age.

Section 2.   The Congress shall have power to enforce this article by appropriate legislation.

Glossary

actual damages Damages that may be proven to be the direct result of a wrongdoing. Example: As a result of a car accident, X has medical bills of $10,000. These are actual damages, provable by a receipt. *Compare* punitive damages.

adulterated Food that is prepared, packed, or held under unsanitary conditions whereby it may become contaminated with filth and/or injurious to health. Also, fraudulent or misleading statements in connection with the preparation and service of foods.

ad valorem A tax based on a total percentage of the value of goods.

affectation doctrine A theory in constitutional law that if intrastate activity (local activity) somehow, even remotely, has an impact on people and/or businesses in another state, then the local activity becomes interstate and thereby subject to the commerce clause.

affirmative defense A defense raised by the defendant that, if proven true, would result in the dismissal of the lawsuit.

animus revertendi Literally means with the "intention to return." One leaves his or her home with this intention or state of mind.

apartment hotels Also a "family hotel" or "residential hotel." Hotels in which apartments are rented for a fixed period of time and include hotel services (maid, linen, secretarial).

apparent authority As a result of actions of the principal (employer), it appears to a third party that an agent has the right to act on behalf of the principal.

[212]

appellant   The party appealing a trial decision. *See also* appellee.

appellee   The party against whom an appeal is taken.

bailment   The transfer of personal property from the owner (bailor) to the bailee for a specific purpose and limited time. Example: Taking clothing to the dry cleaner's creates a bailment. A package left at the hotel front desk (assuming permission of the hotel) is also a bailment.

case law   *See* common law.

cases of first impression   A case before a court for the first time; therefore, the ruling by the court will "make law" in that jurisdiction on a particular issue for the first time.

certiorari   Review by which an appeals court determines whether to hear an appeal. A grant of *certiorari* means the appeals court will review the case, for example. A denial means the decision of the lower court stands.

chattels   Personal property. Property is generally divided into real property (land and all things attached) and personal property (all other types of property). Chattels is a synonym for personal property.

civil action   A court case in which the plaintiff seeks money or an injunction as opposed to a criminal case in which the state seeks incarceration and/or payment of fines.

Clayton Act   A federal law prohibiting price discrimination, exclusive agreements, and mergers where the effect is to substantially lessen competition.

commerce clause   A clause in the U.S. Constitution. See Chapter 4 and Appendix for the full text of the provision.

commercial speech   Speech made by a business, for example advertisements; as opposed to private speech, which is speech made by individuals. The courts have been finding commercial speech protected under the First Amendment, but not to the same extent as private speech.

common carrier   A transporter of goods and/or passengers that is available to the public on a nondiscriminatory basis. Usually held to a high standard of liability for damage or injury.

common law   The body of law based on court (judicial) decisions, whose origin is in England; brought over to the United States to form the basis of American law. Also known as case law.

compensatory damages   Damages that place the nonbreaching party in as good a position as he or she would have been had there not been a breach.

complaint The first pleading (written document) in a lawsuit; the complaint commences the lawsuit.

consideration The theory in contracts that in order to have valid contract formation, it is necessary to have parties obligated to do something they were not previously, legally bound to do. Thus, consideration means that the promisor induced the promisee to do something he or she was not previously, legally bound to do.

contributory negligence Negligence of the plaintiff, offsetting the negligence of the defendant.

defense (to a contract) A legal reason, which, if proven by the defendant, results in a finding in favor of the defendant.

demurrer A pleading filed in court in which a party challenges (questions) the existence of a cause of action. For example, if Ace sues Barber because Ace does not like the color of Barber's sneakers, Barber could file a demurrer stating that the choice of the color of his sneakers is not a legal right given to Ace. In other words, even if the allegations in the complaint are true, there is no legal relief available.

dictum Language in a court case that is not considered law, but rather the opinion of the judge. A statement, remark, or observation.

disaffirmance An act by a minor, before reaching the age of eighteen or within a reasonable amount of time thereafter, in which the minor chooses to avoid a contract.

dissenting opinion In a case (opinion) when a judge disagrees with the majority of the court, the judge may write his or her disagreement and include it in the printed decision. A dissenting opinion is not "law," but a judge's opinion.

Dram Shop Acts Statutes imposing liability upon a bar for the intoxication of a customer that leads to injuries of a third party.

economic adulteration The substitution of less expensive products so as to make a product inferior to what the consumer would have expected.

equal protection The application of laws to all, under like circumstances, pursuant to the U.S. Constitution.

exculpatory clause A contractural agreement in which one of the parties agrees to release the other from any liability for negligence.

executor A person appointed under a will to dispose of property in accordance with the wishes of the deceased.

executory contract A contract in which either or one of the parties has not performed.

exemplary damages *See* punitive damages.

express preemption When passing federal legislation, Congress states as a matter of record that the purpose of their legislation is to take precedence over conflicting state laws.

fiduciary relationship A relationship defined by law as one in which the parties are unequal, and the party with more power has greater legal duties. For example, guardian-ward, attorney-client, trustee-beneficiary.

foreign-natural test Substances found in food that are natural to the food (cherry pit in a cherry pie) are not actionable, whereas foreign substances (glass, worms, metal) are actionable.

franchise A licensing arrangement in which the franchisee has permission to use a trademark, tradename, or copyright license belonging to the franchisor and under specified conditions or limitations.

franchisee The party to whom a franchise is granted.

franchisor The party granting a franchise.

FTC The Federal Trade Commission, a federal administrative agency overseeing, among other things, false advertising.

guest "A transient person who . . . is received at an inn for the purpose of obtaining the accommodations which it purports to offer." *Ticehurst v. Beinbrink* (textbook, p. 110).

holdover A traveler who extends his stay beyond the scheduled duration.

horizontal price fixing Illegally fixing prices among various sectors of business.

implied warranty of fitness for a particular purpose A promise spoken by a seller guaranteeing that the goods will do what the buyer asked.

implied warranty of merchantability An unspoken promise in every transaction involving a sale of goods that the goods are fit for the ordinary purpose for which they were made or purchased. Includes the purchase of food in a restaurant.

inferred preemption When passing federal legislation, Congress did not clearly state its desire to override a state law with which it is in conflict. Nevertheless, if the conflicting state law cannot peacefully coexist with the federal law, the federal law may prevail.

infra hospitium Inside the inn.

injunctive relief A court order to a party to do or refrain from doing something. Example: An injunction was issued ordering the defendant to stop picketing the hotel.

inn "A house where all . . . those who are able and ready to pay for their entertainment, are received, if there is accommodation for them, and who, without any stipulated engagement as to the duration of their stay, or as to the rate of compensation, are, while there, supplied at a reasonable charge with their meals, their lodging, and such services and attention as are necessarily incident to the use of the house as a temporary home." *Cromwell v. Stephens* (textbook, p. 17).

innkeeper   The proprietor of an inn who has the legal obligation to provide lodging and entertainment, for all, at a reasonable price.

insurer of safety   A standard of liability imposed by law on certain businesses in which the business guarantees safety of goods or property.

inter alia   Among other things. Example: "The court stated, *inter alia* . . ." means the court stated many things, of which this is just one example.

interstate commerce   Commerce (business) that crosses state lines.

intrastate commerce   Commerce (business) restricted to within a state's boundaries.

invitee   A person on another's property with permission. The opposite of a trespasser.

judge-made law   Law made by a judge, in a court decision, as the result of litigation or an appeal; as opposed to statutory law, which is made by a state or federal legislature.

judgment   An order by a court to the defendant to pay money to the plaintiff. Example: The court entered a judgment in the amount of $100,000.

licensee   A person invited onto the land of the licensor.

licensor   An owner of land who permits another (licensee) to enter upon the land for a limited time and purpose.

liquidated damages   Damages agreed to in a written contract before the breach takes place. Example: If you do not complete construction of the hotel by September 30, you agree to pay me $1000 per day in liquidated damages.

lodginghouse   A house in which persons are housed for hire for a single night.

misfeasance   Doing an act improperly.

mitigation of damages   A legal duty imposed on a wronged party to lessen or minimize their damages. For example, a wrongfully fired employee has a legal duty to seek employment elsewhere to lessen damages suffered.

motel   A small hotel where lodgings are available for hire, with a minimum of personal services being furnished by the proprietor. Usually there is no distinction between motels and hotels.

Mrs. Murphy's Boardinghouse A building that has five or fewer paying transient guests and is occupied also by the owner.

necessaries Generally, food, clothing, and shelter, but may vary depending on the person's station in life to include automobiles, for example.

negligence A theory of liability in which plaintiff must prove that (1) a standard of care exists (a minimal level of conduct); (2) the defendant fell below the standard (breached); (3) the breach caused the injury (proximate cause); (4) the plaintiff suffered injuries as a result.

negligence *per se* Negligence predicated upon violation of a statute. For example, if a posted speed limit is 35 mph, driving 65 mph is negligence *per se*.

nondelegable Cannot be delegated to another person. Example: The duty of care cannot be delegated (given) to an independent contractor.

nonfeasance Failure to perform an act that one has a legal duty to perform.

offeree The person to whom an offer is made; this person has the power of acceptance.

offeror The person making the offer.

***per se* illegality** Price fixing, regardless of motive. Or division of markets among competitors (to reduce competition); or group boycotts; tying contracts (when the effect is to lessen competition).

preemption doctrine Under the supremacy clause, the doctrine that federal law will supersede state law if that was the intention of Congress.

prima facie Presumed to be true, unless disproved by evidence to the contrary.

private club An organization in which membership is based on selective criteria.

privity A contractual connection between two parties. Example: When A sold towels to B, there existed contractual privity. Lack of privity is sometimes a defense. In the above example, C does not have privity with A or B and therefore may not sue for breach of a warranty.

public accommodation Definition varies depending on state or federal law. Under federal law includes inn, hotel, motel, restaurant, motion picture house, theater, concert hall, sports arena, stadium.

punitive damages Money awarded in a court case to represent punishment of the wrongdoer. Same as exemplary damages.

ratify An act by a minor, upon reaching the age of eighteen, in which the minor chooses to enforce a contract to which he or she is a party; the opposite of disaffirmance.

recission A remedy available in contract law in which the courts restore the parties to the same position they were in before they entered into the contract. For example, if seller and buyer enter into a contract for the purchase of a house, and the seller reneges on the sale, the court could restore the buyer to the position she was in before the contract by giving her back all her money.

remanded A case heard on appeal is ordered back to the trial court for a new trial with instructions from the appeals court.

res ipsa loquitor The legal theory that states if the plaintiff was injured and the instrumentality that injured plaintiff is under defendant's control, then the defendant must be liable.

res judicata "The thing is over"; a court case has been heard and either not appealed or appealed and lost. Once a case has gone through the state or federal court system, to the highest court, the case is over and cannot be heard again.

respondeat superior The theory under which an employer is held liable for the torts of its employees, if the torts are within the scope of employment.

rooming house A building in which furnished rooms are rented on a short-term basis to such persons as the owner chooses to receive.

§1983 Action A federal civil rights statute.

Sherman Act A federal law prohibiting the formation of monopolies.

specific performance An order by a court to a party to perform rather than to pay damages. Does not apply to personal services contracts. Example: The court ordered Maxamillian to transfer the house to Roberta, rather than to pay damages.

stare decisis The legal concept that when deciding a case today, judges must rely on precedent.

state action A federal or state government interest that results in federal law applying to seemingly private activity. Example: Title II, a federal law prohibiting discrimination, applies to private activity (a restaurant) if the restaurant is engaged in interstate commerce.

statutes Laws passed by a federal or state legislature.

supra Above.

supremacy clause   A clause in the U.S. Constitution. See Chapter 4 and Appendix for the full text of the provision.

tort   A civil (private) wrong for which the court may award money damages.

treble damages   Triple damages, awarded in antitrust litigation.

tying contracts   When one contract is dependent on another and results in less competition in the marketplace.

vicarious liability   Liability imposed on one party as the result of the actions of another. *See respondeat superior*, in which the employer is liable for the torts of its employee.

Table of Cases

Index

Air Freight
718 533-4279.